AF431482

GOD

ORDAINED

SLAVERY

VANZELL HOWARD

ISBN 979-8-88943-281-4 (paperback)
ISBN 979-8-88943-282-1 (digital)

Copyright © 2024 by Vanzell Howard

All rights reserved. No part of this publication may be reproduced, distributed, or transmitted in any form or by any means, including photocopying, recording, or other electronic or mechanical methods without the prior written permission of the publisher. For permission requests, solicit the publisher via the address below.

Christian Faith Publishing
832 Park Avenue
Meadville, PA 16335
www.christianfaithpublishing.com

Printed in the United States of America

CONTENTS

The mission and purpose I have been chosen for and have accepted is to write a book on a very sensitive and misunderstood subject of slavery—the physical, the mental, and most diffidently, its spiritual side. But not so much the slavery of the sixteenth and seventeenth century European and American form of immoral, illegal, brutal, inhuman kidnapping, trafficking, and selling practice of slavery condemned by God—the God of Abraham, Isaac, and Jacob, and the Father of our Lord and Savior Jesus Christ. Notwithstanding, there are some parts and practices of slavery that God condoned and ordained for the welfare and the correction of His people, i.e., His children.

CHAPTER 1

God Ordained Slavery

Slavery is a difficult subject to swallow for most human being; especially, for the African American community. They have endured more than two hundred and forty years of hardship from the God-condemned, illegal practices of forced kidnapping, selling, and trafficking of Africans to select parts of the world and especially to America's and Europe's plantations in the past. Unfortunately today, African Americans are still railing from its horrific and damaging effects, but to our chagrin, God has still ordained slavery and servitude all throughout anthropology. Slavery is ubiquitous in the world and to the entire human race—all people, all nations, all tribes, and all kinds have, at one time or another in our human history, operated as slaveholders or lived as slaves in slavery institutions. As long as there is a sovereign, omnipotent, omniscient, omnipresent God and Father as the Lord of Hosts and Master, there will always be servants and children to worship Him. The Father of Glory in heavenly places desires, condones, and ordains slavery and its concept. The thought of a good God—a God of benefits, a God of increase, a God of love, a God of mercy, a God of grace, a benevolent God, a righteous God, the Creator, the Master of the universe, the God of Abraham, Isaac, and Jacob, and the Father of our Lord and Savior, Jesus the Christ—having ordained and condoned slavery is unthinkable. That an invisible, all-powerful God, the Lord and ruler over heaven and earth would come down from His divine seat in glory to humble himself and die like a natural man as a slave to save, to redeem, and to free mankind from the clutches of sin's bondage. Yes, absolutely so! He's a good, just, and righteous God. However, His ways are not our ways and His thoughts are not our thoughts; consequently, it would be difficult for us as mere mortals to comprehend God's grand scheme. Nevertheless, God has given revelation and requests that this subject be discussed and disclosed all around the world. His people need to know that God is revealing a side of himself we don't like to talk about much or just did not want to know. Metaphysical and physical slavery goes back as far as antiquity, even to the very beginning of time with Adam and Eve being under subjection and submission. It is very important to distinguish the differences between the two. *Subjection* is being forced to submit to the authority of another, which is the consequence of the fall of Adam and Eve. In contrast, *submission* is willingly allowing oneself to be ruled by someone or something else you may have deemed an authority in one's life.

How truly, Noah, after the flood, planted a vineyard and allowed a product of the earth—the grape and the vine—to subject him by being under the influence and control of the wine from the vine that put him into a drunken naked stupor. Sounds familiar with the drug-alcohol scene in America and all around the world: an unsober and an irrational people and nation that have submitted themselves to subhuman activity. Noah then perpetuated the ill flash nature and put a curse of subjection on his grandson Canaan, Ham's son, according to the book of Genesis 9:18–29. Noah cursed Canaan and the descendants of Ham to be slaves; that is the first record of a human curse expressed that was issued as a servant to his brethren. This was and still is a human race problem and a family matter. The father and grandfather angry with his son and then cursed his grandson and have become brother against brother, clan to clan confrontation, but by no means was slavery an act of racial superiority or blacks, Negros, Nubians being inferior than white, Caucasian, Aryan people as some would suggest and believe. Moreover, God cursed man and his kind in Genesis because of a lack of discipline and their disobedience to His command; there are two words we, as a race of people, must truly learn to embrace and embody, and they are discipline and obedience. These two words are the essence of life and possessing great faith in God. Truly, loving God is to obey Him as his children and the siblings of Jesus Christ emulating their big brother Almighty's discipline and obedience. The first and last thing God commanded and asked of us was to obey His holy Word and His instructions.

In the book of Genesis 2:16–17, 3:11, God tells Adam not to eat of the fruit of the tree of knowledge of good and evil in the center of Eden's garden, and if you do, it will affect the entire human race. One act of one man, Adam's disobedience, brought the stain of sin and death into the world man's deoxyribonucleic acid—DNA (molecule). Disobedience produces sin, and sin controls this world, and the curse is imputed to us by Adam's inherited disobedient nature. We were born the children of disobedience according to Ephesians 2:3. Disobedience is the root of all humankind's ills and misery flouts and failures!

If you would look at Romans 5:14–21, key verses 18 and 19, you will discover that Paul points out the fact that man and his kind died before the Mosaic law was given in Exodus 20. Adam disobeyed the very voice of God's command, so the offspring will suffer the penalty of sin and not because they deliberately transgressed the law themselves. Paul states that we sinned according to the likeness of the original transgressor, Adam. Paul calls Adam a type, a figure of Christ, and draws the analogy between Adam and Jesus and how they are similar. Adam is a type: he is a production, a pattern, a model of the one who was to come, the Christ Jesus! The similarities of Adam and Jesus are incredible; they both fathered, authored, and headed a characteristic in humanity. Adam fathered the old humanity characterized by disobedience, sin, and death. Jesus our Christ fathered and headed a new humanity characterized by obedience, righteousness, and life. We come under the consequences of Adam's disobedient deed by natural descent; however, we come up under Christ by obedient faith. Adam was tempted in the garden of pleasure and more than enough and still disobeyed the voice of God, the Father of creation; Jesus was also tempted but in the wilderness of lack and need but obeyed the voice of God the Father of glory. Jesus came to restore obedience. The first goal of God's salvation was to cut out the evil root of disobedience and restore man to his original destiny to a life of full obedience to God the Father through Christ Jesus. Another first thing Jesus did was become the second Adam to undo what the first Adam had done. Christ, as the obedient one, saved humankind to be His obedient ones. Disobedience made us mortal, corruptible, and fearful, causing us to stop trusting God and start believing that it was too humiliating to continually do and seek the will of God the Father in our life, as did the prodigal son. You should note the story of the wasteful son as an awesome example of a son's disobedience and falling into despair and coming to himself recognizing and seeing that his father Had slaves living and faring better than he was, and he said to himself, "I will go back to my father and ask for forgiveness of my sins against heaven and my father."

Just to be as one of his servants, one of his slaves in his father's house, you know the rest of the story. The father saw the son from afar and ran and fell on his son, saying, "My son is back. He was dead in sin but has repented and came to himself."

It was known in the Hebrew Churches of that day: if a child dishonored their parent, they could be stoned to death, so the father, being so elated to behold his son, did what any good father would do: covered, saved, and restored him to his right standing as a son with an inheritance. This is why the father ran to the son to get to him before anyone else did, especially the other son. The father told the rest of the slaves to "Go get the best robe, slippers, and a ring, and let's kill the fatted calf as a sacrifice and substitute for my son who was dead and now is alive."

The moral of the parable is that disobedience separates us from the love of God the Father, not that God left us, but we left God the Father to a life of death and destruction, so stay humble, obedient, and patient, and in due season, you will receive your inheritance. Christ came to show us how to put on the robe of humility, which is our humanity. Jesus, the Word of God, came down and prostrated himself, humbled himself, wrapped himself in rags, and laid in an ox stall from glory, from Zion, from that conspicuous place, made himself flesh and took on our nature, our weakness, our shortcoming, and our failures and wore it in obedience to God our Father.

Humanity, as dust, has been deceived to believe we run and control things outside of God the Father's will, and we end up following the counsel of men and the dictates of their own wicked hearts and find ourselves outside the will of God. Jesus also came to overcome and take away our disobedience and to replace it with His own obedience; this is called the gospel of Grace, the good news through Jesus Christ's redemptive work, and it consists of the restoration of obedience to its proper place. That's the beauty of the SALVIFICwork of Jesus Christ that has brought us back to obeying God's voice. God has always used obedient men to save his People: from Noah, to Abraham, to Moses, and to our Lord and Savior Jesus Christ. We must learn to become totally obedient and subordinate to the voice of God the Father, our Creator. For He demands full obedience, for there will not be any entrance into His Glory unless we first obey his voice and commandment. Hear what I am saying: Jesus came to be the head of a people, a kingdom, and a nation prepared with a new and obedient nature as new creatures in Christ. Jesus places supreme importance on obedience; this is the reason He came. Thanks be to God who is rich in mercy because of His great love with which He loved us, even when we were dead in trespasses and sin. He made us alive together with Christ; by grace, we have been saved. Jesus Christ, the last Adam, came to teach us the lost art of heavenly obedience. Only obedience gives man access to the fruitful tree of life and the favor of God. The book of Revelations also reveals the object of God's affections: the blessings He gives to those who keep His commandments that they may have the right to the tree of life. The prophet Jeremiah calls it the benefits of obedience in chapter 7:22–24, "But this is what I commanded them saying, Obey My voice, and I will be your God, and you shall be My people. And walk in all the ways that I have commanded you, which may be well with you. But they did not obey or incline their ears, but followed the counsels and the dictates of their evil hearts and went backward."

This reminds me of the story of the man of God in the book of first Kings chapter 13 who delivered a message from God about the apostasy of the king of Israel, Jeroboam. The man of God was told by the Lord God not to eat bread nor drink water nor return by the same way he came. And he did as the Lord God instructed him to and went another way out of Bethel. However, the man of God was persuaded by an old prophet who pursued the man of God to come back to Bethel to eat bread. The man of God told the prophet that he could not go back nor eat nor drink with him in the place of Bethel because God had commanded him not to. There is death in disobedience. The man of God was convinced and influenced by the prophet because he said an angel spoke to him by the word of the Lord, saying, "Bring him back to eat bread and drink water. The old prophet was lying to him."

And the man of God was torn and killed by a lion that God sent. Disobedience to the Word of the Lord is dangerous (verse 26). Walking in the stubbornness of our imagination and not processing forward the only power we have to obey is in the presence of the voice of God speaking to us; when we understand how great the reward is that God bestows to obedience, you will stop begging and asking for things and be more concerned with hearing and obeying the voice of God the Father and He will take care of the Blessings and the rewards. Our one thought should be, "How can I obey and please God the Father?" God wants to dwell in the midst of his people's obedience. God wants to crown our obedience with His favor and presence. We are to obey from the heart as slaves of righteousness; we are to cast down every imagination, every high thing that exalts itself against the knowledge of God, bringing every disobedient thought into captivity as a slave to the obedience of Christ. Our thoughts and head knowledge leaves us powerless and senseless of God's great ability. We need to recognize our weakness and ignorance of God's will and being conscious of our ignorance will make us more able to understand Jesus' obedience. Obedience is born out of love. John 14:15 and 15:10–14 says, "If ye love me, keep My commandment." The verb *keep* is not imperative, but future those who love Christ will prove their devotion by their obedience and diligently keep God's word and steadfastly abide in His presence.

One man's act of full obedience counteracted and restored obedience, righteousness, and eternal life to all men that believed and obeyed. There is an ancient proverb that I love that illustrates the kind of obedience Jesus desires from the people of God, His body, the church. There was a proud king with a great army demanding the submission of a king over a small but brave nation. The proud king sent an ambassador to the king of the small nation, calling for him to surrender and serve him; however the king over the small but brave and disciplined nation called for one of his soldiers to stab himself in front of the ambassador and the soldier did it at once, and the king called a second soldier and he too obeyed at once, then the king called a third soldier and he too was obedient unto death. Then the king over the small nation told the ambassador, "Go and tell your master that I have three thousand such men. Let him come!"

The king dared to count on men and women who would give up their life when the king would call for it. Think about it: how many of us would do such a thing at the command of the King of Glory? Can God count on you? It is this type of loyalty and obedience that God wants from us. It is this obedience Christ gave; it is this obedience He teaches. We must seek to learn total obedience and nothing less! From the very outset of the Christian journey, let this be our goal and aim. To avoid the fatal mistake of calling Jesus Lord and Master and not doing what He says. So now we toil, we labor, we work, we serve, and we slave all the days of our lives; this is our retribution and our chastisement for Adam's initial sin of disobedience of God's commandment. Humanity has always grappled with obeying and contended with slavery. However, slavery, humility, and meekness will help to transform and convert the mortal anthropoids into becoming sanctified sons of God, the divine children of the Most High God as our Father. This is a metamorphosis that must take place, a change, a removal, and a breaking away of carnality which is a repentant process that we all must go through to receive and understand our purpose in God's great scheme of things for our lives. Therefore, it is our burden as well as our desire as a minister of the gospel of Jesus Christ, as servants of the Most High God, and his slave to love that we can explain how we came to this conclusion. The dynamics of this historical and spiritual event must be broken down into little small pieces for our digestion. Therefore, we need to simplify it by looking at some of the word nuances and their semantic range of words that will help explain this phenomenon. Words that are used in the Bible etymology in grammar and syntax, as well as the Greek, Hebrew, Arabic, and Latin lexicon words to describe the predominant authorities and powers that be. Words such as *God, Lord, king, master, ruler*, etc. For instance, the word *God* is a generic and an abstracted word; it's a general and basic word with no trademark, no brand name. Simply, it has no name. It's vague, theoretical; it's not concrete or real. The God of the universe, the Creator of both heaven and earth, has a name; power and glory is in His name, and He must be magnified which is to be made known throughout the world by His holy and righteous name. Just the expression *god* only denotes a deity or an idol that human beings love to praise and worship. Idols, gods, and deities are anything that humans make with their own hands to worship or honor and adore. We, as human beings, have the propensity, the tendencies, of always making to ourselves gods and idols out of any and everything imaginable; however, there is a true and a living God who has a name, and his name is the Lord of Hosts, Jehovah, Yahweh, Yeshuah, Jesus, Emanuel, meaning God is savior, God with man, God incarnated. The true and living God that operates in the spirit of fatherhood as the loving progenitor, the author and finisher, the maker, and the creator in relationship with his creation, his offspring, his children, his living word, and his workmanship. There is but one true and living God and his name is Yeshua, Jesus the Christ: "At the name Jesus—Yeshua—every knee shall bow, of things in heaven, and things in earth, and things under the earth; and that every tongue should confess that Jesus is Lord, To the glory of God the Father" (Philippians 2:10–11). There is another equal and powerful word, and it is the word Lord. Lord is a word for nobility and of majestic proprietor, those that have control. Yeshua is Lord. He is Lord of lords and King of kings, and the kings are those who are the ruler with domain over his kingdom, the leader and sovereign head of state. Kings serve and are served. Then there are the masters or rabboni, those who operate in supreme knowledge as instructors, doctors, lawyers, and teachers with master's degrees of intellect. Then there are rulers, the ones with complete authority, higher powers, the power that is over and above your power, my power, and all others powers. Deities are the things we honor and worship. Sovereignty, having absolute rule, power, and control over all jurisdiction, then we have the boss, the one in charge of administering in a facility, even the husband is known as the house band, the keeper of order. Finally, yet importantly, we have the argot *shepherd*, the most obscure of all the positions of leadership. The shepherd guards and protects, leads and guides; through thick and thin, through hell and high water, he will do the ultimate by laying down his life for the sheep! Just to name a few major words in this vernacular.

On the contrary, there are also words to describe the prostate being; words like Hebrew *evedh* (slave), Greek *doulos* (servant), *minister, steward, body, bond, humble, base, meek, poor, prisoner, laborer, earthly, flesh, spoil, captive,* and *sheep*—all these words convey lowliness, and all human beings possess some of the nuance of these prostheses. According to the Hebrews custom, slaves could be acquired in a number of ways such as prisoners of war (Numbers 31:7–9), by purchase (Leviticus 25:44), by gift (Genesis 29:24), by debt (Leviticus 25:39), by birth of a slave already possessed (Exodus 21:4), by arrest if the thief could not pay back (Exodus 22:2–3), and by the voluntary decision of the person wanting to be a slave (Exodus 21:5–6).

First and foremost, we must show that a slave is a person that gives his or her will over to another. It may be to the Lord of hosts or a lord of flies, to the one and only true and living God or to a god of wood and stubble, to the Master of the universe or a master of none, to the King of kings or a king of queens. We all are subject to some superior entity, power, and authority in this life because God has ordained it to be so! You are not a slave nor are you a servant, neither are you a steward or minister if you have not surrendered your will over to your higher power; if you are fighting against authority first, our heavenly Father or our human fathers and mothers, then our government official, and our civil servants. You and people with mildness are considered rebels and are the rebellious bodies of disobedient reprobate. From the very beginning of time, God has used unconventional, untraditional, unpopular methods that are not politically correct as far as earthlings are concerned. Foolish things to confound the world's wise, base things and those things that are despised—yes, even slavery! We hate the word *slave*; we deplore it. The saved and the unsaved despise it. This is why God uses slavery for many reasons.

The main reason is to "love," to be a slave is to love. Yes, to serve in love, to love the Lord thy God with all thy heart, with all thy mind, with all thy body, with all thy soul, and with all thy passion and personality. Love is to be worshipped. Love is to be honored, and love is to be praised. For in Christ Jesus, there is neither circumcision nor uncircumcision avails anything, but faith working through love. We will pass from death to life because we are slaves to love, and we love the brethren. We love man and his kind and have learned to love our enemies and forgive them (1 John 3:14). We worship and serve love because God is love, and God is our father and we love God, and every one that loves is of God and knows God. God is love, and if we love one another, God lives in us and his love is made perfect in us, and when we serve God in love, we become a true slave to love, willingly serving God and the brethren in benevolences.

Another good reason for God-ordained slavery is to humble and chasten His people, His children for whom the Lord loves them. He chastens and scourges sons whom He receives. Especially to them who have lifted up themselves in pride, in idolatry, and in disobedience. The people who could but would not humble, submit, or subject themselves to God's will and way. Furthermore, we have had earthy fathers who corrected us, and we paid them respect. Shall we not much more respect and submit to Jehovah God, the Father of life, and live. For indeed, chastisement is only a few days in eternity, but it seems best for it to profit us that partake of God's holiness. But if we are without chastening or corrective discipline of which all have become partakers, then we are considered bastards, rebels, and illegitimate children. It is not joyful now but very painful after it yields the peaceable fruit of righteousness to those who have been trained by it.

God knew that the human race has a problem with being obedient and humble (Adam). God told man and his kind to subdue the earth, i.e., our flesh of dust, our body of clay, our slave man, our selfish self. We, as human beings, are ordained of God. We are called of God, we are predestined of God to master, to defeat, and to have victory over our bodies, our atmosphere, and our society; in the book of Galatians, Paul calls this victory temperance, being strong in a thing, mind over matter, spirit over carnality, love over hate. We must come to the revelation that the body is not saved, but it is a slave, a tool to be used, a working vessel to be manipulated by the glory of God. For the flesh and blood of this body cannot inherit nor enter the kingdom of heaven. The body was made to be submissive and subjected, controlled and used to benefit God's purpose of His incarnation. Look up and examine the word *slave* in your Bible dictionary, the Hebrew correspondent (#5647) and its Greek counterpart (#4983), and you will discover that the human being must be submissive and will be subjected to someone, something, somebody, somehow, somewhere, and most of the time. Whether it be for the good or for the bad, for the right or the wrong, fair or unfair, we were made and ordained to worship, which is simply service as a minister of Jesus Christ!

Looking into the book of Romans chapter 13:1, the scripture says: "Let every soul be subject unto the higher power for there is no power but of God. The powers that be are ordained of God." The powers that be are established by God, and man is set aside and ordered to serve. Let every soul be under subjection. Let every nephesh, let every living being, let every breathing clay nation, let every vital heartbeat depend on the Lord God. Let every thinking mind explore the wonders of God's council. Let every will want holy direction and desire the master touch of wisdom. Let every thought concentrated on its purpose and mission. Furthermore, let every emotion be under the control and power of prudence, and let love have its perfect will of the Father's agape love.

In Jeremiah 27:1–8, God ordered Jeremiah to make a bond and yoke and place them upon his neck. Jeremiah was instructed by God to tell the ambassadors of these nations to convey to their kings that the Lord God Almighty, the God of Abraham, Isaac, and Jacob/Israel, has great power and strength and will put them under the power of God's ordained servant, King Nebuchadnezzar of Babylon. If the nations did not submit to Babylon's king, then God would punish that nation by war, starvation, and disease to destroy it completely. Another example of ordained submission comes from the book of James 4:7, "Submit yourself therefore to God, to Love, resist the devil; the Lyer; the deceiver and he will flee from you."

God ordained slavery. Jesus said in Matthew 6:24, "No man can serve two masters, for either he will hate the one and love the other, or else he will hold to the one and despise the other. Ye cannot serve God and mammon." The thought here is very clear: there will be a master in our lives that we will love or hate and serve the one we love. The great and ultimate and decisive challenge is in our choice against God's will; we have the wonderful opportunity to select between God and mammon, our possession. The Lord of Hosts, the one that controls and rules over all for the good or the one that possesses and oppresses your entire being. The most insidious, beguiling, and pervasive temptation is our love for this world's resources, treasures, and materials. Jesus teaches that the problem with wealth and riches (mammon) is that we become mastered by it when we choose to serve mammon instead of God. God prefers that we have full control and master our money issues. Let us examine Joshua's declaration in Joshua 24:15–24, "And if it seems evil unto you to serve the Lord. Choose you this day whom you will serve. Whether the gods which your fathers served that were on the other side of the flood or the gods of the Amorites in whose land ye dwell; but as for me and my house we will serve the Lord."

The book of Joshua teaches us that the sixth book of the Old Testament was the first book in a group of books called the Former Prophets, and they show the development of Israel. The fulfillment of God's promises of blessing to Israel depending on their cooperation, the blessing of victory, inheritance, abundant provision, peace, and rest all came to the people of God as they obeyed His commandments as well for us today. If you didn't know, God's commandments is to love thy neighbor as thyself. Near the end of the book, Joshua called the people to a life of obedience and faith (22:5–24:15). Today, this abiding trust provides a clear foundation for our growth and blessing, and as surely as blessing follows obedience, judgment follows disobedience. As it did to Achan's sin reveals the principle that no one lives alone (chapter 7), but the sins of one affect the lives of others. The Lord of love, the Lord of Hosts, and the Lord God Almighty revealed the book of Judges, and it also concludes that God, numerous times, sold Israel into slavery and bondage just to bring them into subjection and obedience to Himself. Sadly but truly, adversity, affection, and tragedy allows us to see God in his Newtonian form, in his essence, in his divine nature, in his true love, for God first loves us. First Corinthians 6:19–20 tells us that we are not our own, but we are bought with a price, purchase of God, and His property, His personal servant/slave. Jesus did the ultimate and took on the body of flesh; He humbled himself. Jesus came down from heaven and became a servant, a slave, and obedient to the curse of the cross and the death of the cross (Philippians 2:5–8). The body is a vessel of servitude, and we are to present our bodies as a living sacrifice unto God, holy and acceptable, which is our reasonable, logical, and rational service. This earthen vessel, this clay, this dust, and this dirt, was created and animated for obedience in worship which is our service to the only true and living God Yeshua, our Savior. We, as humans, have actually put too much stock in the flesh, too much pride in life; the body is only good when the Holy Spirit possesses it. We are created unto God for good works and to be rich in good works in the purpose and the way God has before ordained us as his workmanship. Since we are receptacles, vessels, and shells, as the people of God, we must carry within us the knowledge of God the Father. Just as any clay vessel reflects the artisanship of its maker, so do the people reflect the craftsmanship of God the Father and Creator. Man and his kind are clay in the hands of God and are formed in accordance with his plan, for we are his workmanship created in Christ Jesus unto good works. Paul tells us in the book of Philippians 3:34 to "have no confidence in the flesh, i.e., the body, the slave; but in the Lord Jesus Christ."

Once we become submissive to God's will and His way, then agape love starts to saturate our life. The kind of love that gives and gives and gives and gives to the benefit and welfare of others; love is the fulfillment of the law. Charity is God's resolve through humility; the greatest of all his gifts, God's love in action, performing, doing, being obedient to God's commandments, which is to love the Lord God with all our heart and to love one another as thyself. However, love is not a feeling nor is it an emotion! Love is God's sacrificial commitment and his principal responsibility to his creation. God is committed to saving us, regenerating us, edifying us, and God the Father sanctified us as his children. Then and only then can we become a friend of God. Here are three features that make a slave/servant into a friend of God: (1) humility (i.e., humiliation), (2) obedience (i.e., under order) and (3) service (i.e., to hear and to do). John 15:13–15 agrees, "Greater love has no man than this that a man lays down his life for his friends. Ye are my friends if ye do whatsoever I command you. Henceforth, I call you no more servants, for the servant knoweth not what his Lord doeth but I have called you friends for all things that I have heard of my father I have made known unto you. God has chosen us and not us Him, God ordained us to worship."

Our final example is from Philemon; in essence, Philemon had a slave named Onesimus. Philemon's name has a significant meaning that comes from the Greek root word "philo," which means "love"; like in the messianic word Philadelphia, brotherly love. The name Philemon is also a derivative of "philio," which also means "friendly." In the book of Philemon, there is a very interesting and fascinating look into slavery and Christianity that illustrates to us how God established His dynamics for our sanctification of human growth. This story has Philemon representing and symbolizing the master (God) and Onesimus represents all slaves, rebellious and sinful run away. Onesimus's name means "profitable," even though at this time, he is a runaway slave and very much unprofitable. Onesimus met up with Paul the apostle. The Bible does not say how Paul converts Onesimus to Christianity or how Onesimus became saved, born again. Nevertheless, Paul loved Onesimus like a son; he became very useful to Paul, but Paul knew he could not keep Onesimus. After all, he was a runaway slave, and Paul had to send him back to his master. Paul wrote a personal letter, a prayer of sorts, to Philemon to intercede on behalf of Onesimus for his safety. The letter says, "To

Philemon, a good master, do not treat Onesimus as the customs of the Romans do to runaway slaves by beating or killing them."

Paul is now in the position of Jesus the Christ. Paul tells Philemon, "If Onesimus owes you anything for your loss, I will pay." Here is redemption, salvation, and justification; redemption as Paul's whole mission was to reveal Christ's purpose for dying on the cross was to purchase humanity back and liberate man and his kind from the oppression of Satan's lies, from sin, and from the legalistic religious hypocrisies. That's true emancipation—to serve the true and living God of Glory. Salvation is to God the Father for the world He so loves, Jesus came to rescue and recover the children of God the Father. Then there is our justification Christ made for us through his death and blood, excusing us, validating, and explaining our sins away through faith in Jesus as the Christ the Savior of the world. The love, the grace, and the mercy of God so cherished the world that he gave his only begotten son that whoever believed in Jesus as the Christ shall not perish but shall have everlasting life. Therefore, Paul stands in the image of Christ; he would save an unprofitable slave like you and me while we were yet sinners. Christ died for the ungodly—yes, even you and me to become believers in Christ Jesus, useful and profitable to God and man. I am not trying to be correct grammatically, theologically, philosophically, politically, or otherwise; my attempt is to reveal the unpredictable, the undesirable, the unfamiliar, the unnatural, and the unusual character of God the Father. God's word then and His work now is still a wonder to perform; He works in mysterious ways!

In conclusion, in the book of Matthew 23:8–12, it states:

> But be not ye called rabbi: for one's your master even Christ; and all ye are brethren, and call no man your father upon the earth for one is your father, which is in heaven, neither be called master: for one is your master, even Christ, but he that is greatest among you shall be your servant. Whosoever shall exalt himself shall be abased and he that shall humble himself shall be exalted.

God ordained slavery, the principle of greatness and humility; staying low, obscure, and working and God will raise you up. Hallelujah! To God be the glory! The word of God reverberates in the book of Luke 12:48b, "For everyone to whom much is given, from him much will be required; and to whom much has been committed, of him they will ask the more." To those who have the greater knowledge of truth will be held accountable for the wise stewardship of that knowledge. If you are a boss, an owner, a teacher, a preacher, or some great and affluent person, you, in essence, are the ones that must do the heavy lifting. Congressmen, senators, governors, mayors, and as well as the president, you guys are the minister and the servants! God has blessed you with His glory to look out for and to protect the little children, i.e., the less fortunate.

Jesus warns the scribes and Pharisees and the audience against pride and seeking of public praise and attention made obvious by their desire for places of status and titles suggesting to be superior. The titles themselves may be used as terms of respect or to indicate certain duties and places of responsibility; however, it is the attitudes behind the seeking of such titles and recognition that Jesus condemns. Watch your attitude for lofty ambitions. As believers of the gospel of Jesus Christ, we are peculiar and owe our reverence to Christ alone.

Jesus continued to issue a series of dreadful warnings and condemning criticism by charging the scribes and Pharisees of being hypocrites and frauds. Not only did the Pharisees and scribes refuse the truth of the Gospel of Jesus as the Christ, but also by their superstitious legalism, they created barriers and walls to keep those who were seeking the truth from finding it. While professing righteousness, they were unjust in their conduct, and they were found out to be obsessed missionaries of evil works. They became habitual liars, betraying their moral compass, lacking in common sense, developing elaborate and ridiculous systems of ordinance, and making oaths they considered mandatory but were not necessary. They were blatantly contradictory, having lost all sense of direction in the consequence of spiritual issues that matter. They remind me of the reality show, *Preachers of L.A, Detroit, and Atlanta*, betraying their moral and humble disposition for filthy lucre by constantly misleading of the people of God, calling right wrong and wrong right, and are just full of pride and worldly lust running over and then have the unmitigated gall telling us this is the will of God. First Timothy 6:10–16 tells us about a good confession: it states that the man of God must fight the good fight of faith and lay a hold to eternal life. We must flee these worldly things—the love of money and the pride of life with its deceptive lordship—and pursue after righteousness, the way of God; pursue after godliness, the will of God; pursue after faith, the hope of God; pursue after love, the mercies of God; pursue after patience, the endurance of God; and last but not the least, pursue after gentleness, the care and compassion of God.

You can't convince me of the buffoonery of our twenty-first century scribes, Pharisees, and clergymen. This is some old mess that's been going on for years and a day. Vain men stop the charade we all have been exposed and have become transparent. Man can see right through the façade; it is crystal clear. Let's just confess our sins to God for He is faithful and just to forgive us of our sins and cleanse us from all unrighteousness; this is the power of the word of God. Do you believe it? Trust in the Lord thy God with all thy heart and lean not to thy own understanding but in all thy ways (the good and the bad) acknowledge the Lord, and He will direct thy pathways and will sanctify your life.

Part 2
God Ordained Government/Slavery
Romans 13:1–7 KJV

Our thought and theme derives from the thirteenth chapter of the book of Romans, and Romans is an extraordinary epistle. The author and writer is the one and only Paul the apostle, a slave he would call himself, and a prisoner of the Lord Jesus Christ, a Hebrew of Hebrews with Roman citizenry. However, when Paul wrote the book Romans, he had not yet been to Rome. He wrote to the church of Rome to introduce himself to its people he was eager to visit and meet. Paul most likely wrote the book of Romans while incarcerated in a Corinth jail around AD 56, declaring to be a prisoner of Christ. This epistle is therefore a complete declaration of his understanding of the gospel of Jesus Christ and is considered the greatest illumination of Christian doctrine anywhere in scriptures. This epistle contains a systematic order of logical and reasonable growth of profound theological truths: that we are to be patient, we should rejoice, we must grow, we must keep hope alive, we must walk in love, we must pray insatiably, we must praise God at all times, and trust in His Word. Romans is filled with the great themes of redemption: the guilt of all mankind, our inability to earn favor with God, the redeeming death of Christ, and the free gift of salvation to be received by faith alone.

The book of Romans teaches us that we should not trust in ourselves for salvation, but that we need to trust in our Lord Jesus Christ and imitate the faith of Father Abraham. In addition, put all our hope in the glory that Lord God will bring good out of trouble, joy out of pain, love out of fear/hate, and peace out of confusion that we might represent our Lord and Savior, Jesus the Christ. The book of Romans continues to show us that we should grow in our daily dying to sin and self that promotes our walking in the spirit.

However, other Christians not mentioned in scripture have founded the church in Roman, but Paul came to know many of them that believed there throughout his travels, and Phoebe, a companion, likely delivered the letter to the church in Rome. When Paul was arrested and was about to be beaten to death in Jerusalem, he requested to see Caesar calming his Roman citizenry as a Jew born in Tarsus of Cilicia. This citizenship trumps all other nationalities and resembles the kingship and residency of heaven and our new birth. And on the voyage to Rome, Paul became shipwrecked and had many near-death experiences. It was a miracle that he even truly arrived in Italy to be tried in the Roman court. But there was such a great backlog and a gridlock in the Roman juridical system that Paul spent two years living in a guarded residence with free access to go and come and minister as he pleased: look at God. Paul began evangelizing, preaching, and teaching the word of God, the Gospel of Jesus Christ, to the Hebrews and Roman citizens while imprisoned in Rome, God's providences. Paul wrote our epistle's cyclical letter, one to be read by several church congregations like the ones in Ephesians, Philippians, Colossians, and Philemon. Paul's doctrine agreed and coincided with that of Doctor Luke's historical and analytical recording in his gospel. Chapter 2 of Luke proclaims that Christ Jesus was born in the time the Roman Emperor Augustus Caesar reigned and when the Romans controlled the world's climate and its people. When Gaius Octavius, the great-nephew of Gaius Julius Caesar who adopted Octavian and made him his heir. After the assassination of Julius Caesar, Gaius Octavius became coruler of Italy along with Mark Antony, and after the demise of Mark Antony and Cleopatra, Octavian became Caesar over all of Italy and made

Rome the capital city and pronounced himself to be a deity and took on the name and title of Augustus Caesar, Latin for "majestic ruler," Caesar, "King," from 30 BC until AD 14. In addition, Augustus Caesar made a decree that all the world (his kingdom, the Roman empire) was to be census and needed to registered for the purpose of taxation, and the census was first taken while Quirinius was governor of Syria during 10–7 BC and later served a second term during AD 6–9 (Anno Domini is Latin for "in the year of our Lord"). That the head of each family journeyed back to their hometown where their ancestral records were kept.

When Jesus arrived on the scene, His birth became the demarcation of dividing time/*kairos* and seasons/*chronos*, dispensation, and millennium and designates a fixed or special occasion, which denotes a particular period. Jesus's life, death, burial, and resurrection was and is the connection, the bridge, that links time and eternity, the physical with the spiritual, and the old covenant to the new covenant, reconciling God and man back together in peace through the grace of God and the faith in Jesus as the Christ. This is grace and truth. The Israelites were under the authority of the kingdom of Roman sovereignty and were slaves, colonized Roman citizens, and Israel was an occupied settlement. According to Paul's epistle to the Galatians 4:4–5, it conveys that God sent his son in the fullness of time when the conditions of the world favored the appearance of Jesus the Christ! Paul elaborates on Jesus Christ being the anointed king of glory, the very son of God the Father. His humanity, Jesus being born of a woman, and his subjection and obedience to the law and even to death—all that means is that Jesus was obedient and subjected to serve as a slave. He was wrapped in swaddling clothes, simply wrapped in rags and laid in a manger in a lowly ox stall and was first recognized and accepted by shepherds or low, disregarded slave workers. Then they escaped to Egypt (the land of bondage) and then exodus out of Egypt like a runaway slave to freedom as a new son, then He went to live in a poor slightly obscure village called Nazareth. Raised as a carpenter, then He started to build the kingdom of God here on earth; nevertheless, He stayed humble, calling men of like manner, from zealots to farmers to fishermen to thieves to publicans to prostitutes, socially considered low-lifers and sinners. Jesus continued on in the role of a slave, living without a place to call his home ("no place to lay His head") and then arrived at the ultimate act of humiliation as the Master of the universe, washing the feet of His very own disciples and followers. The dissension proceeds: Jesus then takes a ride on the back of a lowly ass colt of an undomesticated donkey into Jerusalem as the king of the Jews, but He's really on His way to Calvary's cross to die like a natural criminal slave for the human race. Let it be known that no sin or Gould was found in Him, but He stayed steadfast in obeying the will of the Father. They beat our Lord and Savior all night long like a criminal slave, and He did not say a mumbling word, then they nailed our God to that old rugged cross for your sins and mine. He sacrificed and died the way slaves do. They laid Him in a borrowed tomb like a slave, but to God be the glory, in three days, He got up! With all power in His hands, He fulfilled the love of God through loving obedience! Therefore, when the fullness of time came, God sent forth His Son, born of a woman, born under the law, to redeem those who were under the curse of the law, that we might receive the adoption as sons. God's purpose in sending Jesus was to rescue the lost souls and to lose the enslaved of their fleshly bonds to salvation by redeeming us to Himself and to bring all slaves into sonship through adoption. For we did not receive the spirit of bondage to fear anymore, but we are now free children. We have received the spirit of adoption and the assurance that we are God's sons and daughters, whereby we call Abba Father/Daddy God! God has allowed us to have an intimate relationship with Him and to get to know Him in a very real way through the Holy Spirit and His son Jesus and the Trinity will relate to those who are heirs, and we are then able to call out to God by the Spirit.

The condition of the world was at its full zenith for whenever men exalted themselves to become a majestic deity, as did Octavian Caesar. God has the tendencies and a way of transcending our hemisphere and atmosphere and dominion, making sure that humankind stays humble, and when they went too far, God would reach out and touch them by intercepting their misunderstanding. For instance, men like Nimrod, renowned to be a mighty hunter in the land of

Babylon. The people started to praise him, and he began to believe that he was God. So the Lord God, the Sovereign One, had to step down out of heaven's glory to encounter him and the Babylonian people by confusing their language and understanding of the people. In addition, men like Pharaoh who believed he was the sovereign god; you know the story how the Lord God, the Great I Am, the Immovable Mover, showed up and showed out with ten overwhelming and persuasive plagues, destroying all the gods in Egypt and to say, "I Am the Lord thy God, the Master of the universe."

Nebuchadnezzar was another earthling that came to self-aggrandizement, thinking that he too should be a deity as he looked out over the kingdom that the Lord God gave to him in all its glory for a season, and Nebuchadnezzar said, "Look at what I have made." This story also is well-known as previously mentioned how the Lord God redirected and changed the course of the old king's life with an immediate transformation into a beast for a prior of seven years, just to catch his complete attention so that he would know and recognize that the Lord God of Israel, the Most High, rules in the kingdom of men and gives it to whomever He will and sets over it the lowest of men is also the Lord God of Daniel a.k.a Belteshazzar, as well as the God of Hananiah a.k.a Shadrach, Mishael a.k.a Meshach, and Azariah a.k.a Abed-Nego and is the true and living God that rules and reigns in both heaven and earth. He is the God that restores, and God restored Nebuchadnezzar back to his position as king, and the kingdom of Babylon was still the same way it was when he lifted it. Ain't God Alright? The most astonishing thing is how Gaius Octavius Caesar promoted himself to Augustus Caesar. This time, the culmination of time, season, and worlds have come together. The Romans had a kingdom that resembled what the Lord God had ordained when He established His kingdom and government method.

"Let every soul be subject unto the higher powers. For there is no power but of God: the powers that be are ordained of God" (verse 1 NLT). Obeying the law is also obeying government authority and all sovereign kingship have been approved and establish by God, the Father of Lights, the Lord God of Abraham, Isaac, and Jacob, and the Father of our Lord and Savior, Jesus the Christ, the Master of the universe. The kingdom of heaven and the kingdom of God are synonymous, yet still there is a demarcation involved; for instance, the kingdom of heaven is the location of God's residence. It's a position, it's upward bound, it's over the top. The kingdom of heaven is the apex, the summit, the zenith, the climax, the pinnacle, and is exalted above all else. On the other hand, the kingdom of God is wherever there is energy/force, wherever there is wind/breath, and wherever there is matter/ molecule. God is there and has rule, domain, kingship, and authority; it could be up or down, heaven or hell, east or west, or in the hearts of man and his kind. Moreover, since He, God, the Father of lights, is omnipresent and omnipotent, He is everywhere at the same time with all power and fills all space and time; this is the kingdom of God. However, the kingdom of heaven is God's paradigm and the first of its kind, the model of what the world's kingdoms, governments, and authority should look like and imitate. For God has ordained and ordered fellowship, leadership, and headship. God alone commanded it to be so, for He is the Alpha and Omega, the First and the Last, the beginning and the end. The I Am that I Am; God is the progenitor, the one who founded all authorities, all powers, all principalities, all governments, all kingdoms, and all nations, to be in obedience. Vr.2 KJV Whosoever therefore resists the power, resists the ordinance of God: and they that resist shall receive to themselves damnation (verse 2 NLT) so those who refuse to obey the laws of the land are refusing to obey God, and His punishment will follow.

To ordain is to establish something, to place somebody, and to appoint someone officially to a purpose; it is a command or order a mission by law, to design, and to predestine, and to intend. God the Father intended for mankind to obey Him, His Word/Jesus, His laws/the Holy Spirit, and his wonderful works of miracles that God ordained and appointed. The Lord God of glory ordained government to function as its own sovereignty, standing alone with no alliance to anybody but Yeshua, our Lord and Master. Through obedience and service, we are ordered to serve the Lord God and humanity, the ultimate in love and honor. Paul, the apostle of Jesus Christ, exhorts us to read the whole oracle of God and fully honor and love the Lord thy God in obedience to the kingdoms and governments He has ordained and established from the foundation of the world. The authorities that exist are appointed by God; let us examine the book of Daniel 4:28–32. King Nebuchadnezzar saw the hand of God's miraculous power and believed in the Spirit of the Holy God that gave Daniel the ability to interpret dreams; however, the king was still full of pride, the one thing that keeps us separated and out of the will of God the Creator. King Nebuchadnezzar was one that loved to boast and brag about his mighty powers and how he built up Babylon, not realizing that God has all power, all authority, and total dominion and allowed, called, and appointed him His servant to enslave, reign, rule, and chase Israel. Therefore, humiliation must have its place in the life of King Nebuchadnezzar and in us as well as long as we continue in a proud and arrogant spirit. God's judgment had to come down on those who neglect, disobey, and resist His command to serve. The prophecy Daniel spoke came to pass and failed on King Nebuchadnezzar and he became insane. He literally lost his natural mind, and the kingdom was taken away from him and he was driven out from the very society over which he had ruled. Nebuchadnezzar began to act and behave like a wild animal, eating grass and walking on all fours, hair turned into feathers all over his body, and fingernails grew like claws, and this condition went on for seven complete years. Until King Nebuchadnezzar realized and recognized that the God of heaven is the King of glory, the Master of the universe, and the Lord of Hosts! Nebuchadnezzar came to know Jesus as the Son of God, the fourth person in the fiery furnace, the King of kings, the Lord of lords, and the God of gods, the Immovable Mover! Nebuchadnezzar, at the end of the time allotted, came to his senses and his understanding, being enlightened, returned to give God the glory and the praises He so rightly deserved, for God's dominion is an everlasting dominion and His kingdom is from generation to generation. All the inhabitants of the earth are reputed as nothing; God does according to His own will in the army of heaven, and no one on earth can restrain His hand or say to Him, "What are you doing?"

The restoration of King Nebuchadnezzar was designed to show God's ideal for all rulers to surrender their kingship unto God's ultimate control. God ordained obedience, submission, and subjection to earthly authority as the general ideal. A clear biblical principle is that we may need to disobey the government if commanded to sin against God's word, for loyalty to God always takes priority over all human authority. The powers and authorities that exist are appointed by God; however, Paul does not suggest that God approves of corrupt governments and ungodly leaders or unjust officials. Sometimes, God will use them to His expected end. God punishes people because of their sins or for other reasons known to Him. God allows evil rulers to have power for a season to humble them. He loves and chastises. Ideally, God grants authority to serve the greater good, and authority is exercised and will be the accounted to each of them to whom it has been given.

When government agencies use force to restrain, discipline, and punish the evildoer, they are not doing wrong, rather they are doing the will of God as ministers and servants of the gospel of Jesus Christ, as well as Christians, should not worry about serving in the government as soldiers and police officers with a good conscience. God gives us two reasons why we, as Christians, must obey government laws and orders. First, because of the wrath of God: this is why we should avoid the punishment that the government executes on those who are wrongdoers for conscience's sake. This is because we want to keep a clear mind before God, who has established all governments and principalities and has commanded us to obey them. Slavery laws that we had to obey in the old days so men and women fought for the right to change the laws that they thought was not good for the country. The second reason God meant for us is that even where there is no likelihood of arrest or punishment, we, as Christians, should be fully obedient to government that He ordained.

The Separation of Church and State

The church, the body of believers, the assemblies of God, together as a group of called-out, elected Christians designed to represent the body of Christ, saved sinners, regenerated saints of the grace of Jesus Christ, disciplined disciples of the word of God cautioning others and safeguarding sound teaching in love. The English derivative of the word *church* comes from the Greek word *ekklesia*, hence *ecclesiastical* or *congregation* from the Old Testament, the gathering of the disciples of Jesus Christ. The church has its nativity on the day of Pentecost with faith in the resurrection of Jesus Christ, and from the outset, the church has both a local and a general significance, denoting both the individual assembly and the worldwide community. Nowhere in scripture does the word "church" identify a place or an edifice of worship, but rather a group of human beings as a body of believers, trusting in Christ Jesus, and only a few times—three to be exact in the New Testament. Christendom also has a two-fold usage that leads us to the consideration that the church is not primarily a human structure like a political, social, or financial organization. Jesus Christ called the church His in Matthew 16:18. He said "My church," the organism, not an organization as the old folk would say. Jesus being the chief cornerstone of the foundation of the holy kingdom of living stones of the living God. It is the fellowship of saints, the people of God, and it is considered the bride of Jesus the Christ as a living organism. The church is apostolic, for it rests on the foundation of the prophets and apostles; the apostles are the first authoritative leaders whose testimony and witness is based on the teaching and calling of Jesus Christ. The church function continued to draw its life from Jesus the Christ through the Holy Ghost (Spirit) and the word of God; from it, we get life and life more abundant and eternal glory.

Now the state is the body that governs the people within any given area. It operates at the national or federal level, the regional or state level, and the local or municipal level. To be able to govern and rule, the state must have the right to rule and the rulers must be accountable to someone. The state must also have laws and the authority to punish those who break the laws. The government must also be relatively stable; that is, it should be able to exist for some time. The relationship between the organism of the bodies of Christ and the organized political state working together for the Bible makes it clear that the right to rule is not rooted in the consent of the governed or the government, but it derives from Jehovah, God Almighty, Yahweh. Rulers are thus accountable to Him, the Lord

God, even if they refuse to acknowledge this fact of truth. The state is to protect all its citizens, administer punishment, restrain evil, and promote peace, justice, and the general welfare of its citizens. Some Christians disagree on the correct relationship between the church and the state, arguing for separation. While others view the church and the state as unique institutions with different functions and roles that should not interfere with each other's sovereignty. However, there are others like myself, and particularly those in the mainstream denominations, that support transformation and argue that Jesus Himself came to transform and resurrected lives and governments and to show us that Christians are called to exert a godly influence on the state and in society and transform it on the basis of biblical values and principles. This attitude even led to a situation like that in Zambia, where former President Chiluba declared it a Christian nation. You also have nations like Rome and America that were influenced by Christianity. Good government must comply with God's laws that govern his creation and humanity. Thus, every state should recognize its moral accountability to God and its citizens and the solidarity and equality of everyone within the state. States should also honor and respect the freedoms that citizens have enjoyed and that are necessary for effective political and economic development and participation. Recognizing the reality of their own limitations and the power of sin, states must also be willing to place limits on financial and political power in order to prevent such power being abused.

The Bible sees the church and the state having three main purposes in relationship:

1. The church must pray for those in authority and for the protection and healing of the nation (1 Timothy 2:1–5): "Therefore I exhort first of all that supplications, prayers, intercessions, and giving of thanks be made for all men, for kings and all who are in authority, that we may lead a quiet and peaceable life in all godliness and reverence, for this is good and acceptable in the sight of God our Savior, who desires all men to be saved and to come to the knowl-

edge of the truth. For there is one God and one Mediator between God and men, the Man Christ Jesus."

2. The priestly purpose. The church must provide teaching, counseling, and direction to the authorities and to those governed (Matthew 28:19–20): "Go therefore and make disciples of all the nations, baptizing them in the name of the Father and of the Son and of the Holy spirit, teaching them to observe all things that I have command you; and lo I am with you always, even to the end of the age."

3. A pastoral purpose. The church should encourage Christians to be good citizens who obey the authorities and pay their taxes/tithes and assessments. The church must rebuke and oppose the state when it turns against God or acts unjustly. When it comes to a confrontation between Christian and political leaders (Acts 5:29, a prophetic purpose): "But Peter and the other apostles answered and said: We ought to obey God rather than men."

Our absolute obedience must be to God such obedience will cost you.

Manasseh Restored after Repentance

Now when he was in affliction, he implored the Lord his God, and humbled himself greatly before the God of his fathers, and prayed to him; and He received him entreaty, heard his supplication, and brought him back to Jerusalem into his kingdom. Then Manasseh knew that the Lord was God. (2 Chronicles 33:12–13)

Father God, in the name of Jesus Christ of Nazareth, our King, my prayer is that we will humble ourselves greatly before Thy mighty hand, hear and receive our supplication and restore us back to your glory. Amen.

CHAPTER 2

Subdue and Dominion
Genesis 1:27–28

> So God created man in His own image; in the image of God He created him; male and female He created them. Then God blessed them, and God said to them. Be fruitful and multiply, fill the earth and subdue it; have dominion over the fish of the sea, over the birds of the air, and over every living thing that moves on the earth.

God made male and female in His image to bear His essence in the earth; man and woman (Adam: ah-dalm, man, mankind, Adam the first man, humanity at large). Adam is translated "Adam;" his proper name is mentioned about twenty times in the Old Testament and is translated "man and his kind" (mankind, humanity) more than five hundred times. When referring to the whole human race, the Bible often uses the phrase "B'nay' Adam," the children of Adam. As the English word *man*, Adam, in its general sense, has nothing to do with being a male or maleness, but everything to do with humanity and humanness. For example, in one case, Adam referred exclusively to women in the book of Numbers 31:35. Adam can be referred to and related to the verb "Adom," ruddiness or red of man's complexion. Adamah, "soil" or "ground," may also be derived from this verb.

Thus, Genesis 2:7 saying the Lord God formed Adam of the dust of the ground. Psalm 103:14 states, "For God knows our frame and He remembers that we are dust." Adamah = earth, man = earthy. Man and woman, male and female, are made in the image and the likeness of the Lord God. The Bible tells us in the book of Matthew that God the Father is a spirit and cannot be defined by man, for God neither is an object nor is He a species; there are no limits, no categories, no reality, which transcends measurement in space and time to fit God. God is the uncreated source; incomparably alive; insurmountable in knowledge, power, presence, and personality; an eternal spirit who is holy, lovely, who creates, sustains, and governs all things. He is the Great I Am!

From the very beginning, the Lord God's heart was to build a kingdom of anthropomorphs, a house of terrestrial souls, a tabernacle of earthlings, a people, a nation, a vessel as His dwelling place on earth's mundane shores that He would be seen in His creation. Man and woman, male and female, together the foundation of the Lord's kingdom through the two of them together procreating, being fruitful, multiplying, and replenishing the earth. This was commanded by God a few times and even spoken to Noah and his sons in Genesis 9. God the Father has commanded and ordained the male and the female to engage in marriage, which is the marrying, the amalgamation, the merging, the mixing, the blending, the whipping, the beating, and the pounding together of two hunks of clay into one. This is the consummating activities to produce one out of two, two becoming one, and their offspring, their children of the same like mind in fellowship with God the Father. The very first miracle Jesus performed was at an insufficient wedding in Cana of Galilee, changing water into some of the very best wine; wine is symbolic of joyfulness. "Thy cup runneth over." Psalm 104:15 says, "Wine that makes glad the heart of man." Proverbs 31:6 says, "Wine to those who are bitter of heart." Ecclesiastes 10:19 says, "Wine makes merry," for the joy of the Lord is our strength. The symbolism of wine is very important to the rigid course of matrimony; it also introduces the power of the Holy Spirit in keeping together, smoothing out, and sanctifying the union unto God the Father, then it became holy matrimony.

The male: the man, masculine, virile, mature, strong manhood, the seed of the sexes that begets offspring by the insemination and the fertilization of the female. Wombman. The female: the woman, the receiver of the fertilizing organ seed, the egg bearer, the incubator, the sex that begets offspring by hollowing the womb of life, feminine, strong, mature, vibrant womanhood. God the Father designed His way and only His way to produce and increase life on earth through the man and the woman, the male and the female of all species of His creation.

If we were to use the science of electrical energy to ascertain God's ultimate purpose of the character of man and woman, you will discover what scientists call the positive and negative charge to produce energy or power, light, and/or life. One kind of charge is positive (+) and the other kind negative (-), also known as like and unlike charges. In the *Compton's Encyclopedia* (A Britannica Publication) it states that electricity "is the servant of modern man." It also states how the theory of electricity works. There is static and electric charge; no one has ever seen electricity as one can see a steam of water or the flame in fire; however, we can watch how it acts in the form of static electric charge. Static electricity can be seen at work when hair is combed on a dry and cold day as well as how the experiment of the comb and wool or a glass rod with silk is rubbed together shows how something happens when held near the pitch balls. Once the pitch ball touches the comb or the rod, it flies away and is simply repelled, because portions of the same (or like) kind of charge repel each other. It is a rule and a law of nature that like electric charges repel each other—positive (+) and positive (+) or negative (-) and negative (-)— and it is unnatural for same likeness to produce anything right or of power. Since the comb and the glass rod both repel the ball, it would seem the both have the same kind of charge. Another experiment shows that this is not true. Two pitch balls are used for this test. One is charged by touching it to a rubbed comb and the other to a rubbed glass rod. If the balls are brought close together, they attract each other. This means that the charges must be unlike or a positive and a negative charge, since they would repel each other if they were alike. It is therefore a rule and a law of nature that unlike electric charges attract each other. Thus, the experiment proves two rules: (1) like charges repel each other two positive or two negative, and (2) unlike charges attract each other, positive and negative.

The man—the male—is considered to be the negative charge (-), the electrical charge produced by rubbing glass with silk. DC, direct current, the steady flow of electrons flowing in one direction—only this relates to the male man. The woman—the female—is considered the positive charge. The AC (alternating current), changing directions 120 times each second. The positive (+) exists on particles called protons, and one or more protons form the center, or nucleus, of every atom. Each proton has a positive charge exactly equal in strength to the negative charge on one electron. Attraction between the unlike charges hold the protons and the electrons together in the atom, producing power, energy, and life. Look at God; this is awesome how the ruler of the cosmic and the earth worked His wonderful, intelligent creation, His masterpiece, man and his kind, as a great part of nature and its makeup—man—in order to maintain the earth by subdue and dominion the atoms, DNA carrier of genetic code: polymer, molecules, and RNA—ribonucleic acid.

God intended to live, reveal, and manifest His glorious character in them on the earth, expressing His dominion over all creation. Man has a basic intrinsic value; the human worth is his divine destiny to be God's agent and God's image and likeness on earth and in the world. The spiritual side of man is prominent in the order of creation. Man's intellect, perception, and determination far exceed that of any other being. Man and his kind have the capacity, the ability, the accountability, and the responsibility to rule with controlling and authoritative power over the earth and in the world, and to do less is to be an unfaithful and unprofitable stewards-managers of our life and precious talent God has entrusted to us.

Verse 28 tells us to be fruitful and multiply; that means "Adam," both male and female, man and woman, positive and the negative sparking energy, husband and wife, bearing and producing many children, to progenerate offspring, to produce seeds, to plant a garden of faithful believers, stewards-managers, and worshipers to love the Lord God our Father by filling the earth with your life so that you can have power to fight against everything in it that leads to death, rule with care and fairness over the natural world, over all of God's beautiful creation, including the aggressive satanic forces which would soon infringe and rear its ugly head. This is why we need to embrace the word and the concept of subdue. *Kabash* is Hebrew for "to subdue or to enslave;" hence, we subdue the earth because without subjugation, the harshness of nature would produce death to mankind. Subdue implies that God has an element of surprise in creation that warrants Him blessing us. God's command for us to subdue and have dominion was for man and his kind to bring creation into submission by knowledge, power, strength, persuasion, and ability, and it will be subdued and this is the promise of Micah 7:1–9, saying he will subdue our iniquity. As God subdues that which is in us sin, so we too subdue our nature that leads to death: to have life in God eternal. Our obligation still remains; the presence of sin complicates matters but does not remove our obligation.

Jesus' words in the book of John 15:1–8, "I am the true vine, and my Father is the gardener (the husbandman). He cuts off every branch that doesn't produce fruit, and he prunes the branches that do bear fruit so they will produce even more. You have already been pruned for greater fruitfulness by the message I have given you to remain in me, and I will remain in you. For a branch cannot be fruitful apart from me. I am the vine, you are the branches; he who abides in Me and I in him, he bears much fruit, for apart from Me you can do nothing. If anyone does not abide in Me, he is thrown away as a branch and dries up; and they gather them and cast them into the fire and they are burned. But if you abide in Me, and My word abide in you, ask whatever you will, and it shall be done unto you. My Father is glorified by this that you bear much fruit, and so prove to by My disciples."

These verses provide the beautiful truth of God's given abiding dominion, the example in which God subdues sin by pruning and cutting it away; using the sower, the farmer's way of subduing nature and the earth through agriculture, reaping and sowing, we have the power and the ability to be the husbandmen. Controlling the conditions problem: solvers whose aim is to improve the visual landscape of our community and all other living creatures that gives man fulfillment in God's commands to subdue by abiding in Jesus, the Word of God, experiencing growth, maturity, and productivity for the kingdom of God by bearing fruit. Loving God the Father is to keep His commandments and rejecting our desire to become independent from God. Nurture an increasingly deeper relationship with Jesus Christ just as Jesus did by keeping His Father's word. When we abide in Christ, our prayers are effective, and we demonstrate our discipleship and authority, as well our joy is complete. That's subduing and dominion.

Then we can have dominion over the earth. The word *dominion* or *to rule* is a Hebrew word (*radah*) meaning "royalty, dominating ruler of a king," but before you think from man's perspective, let's pause and look at God's perspective. Let's think of the King of kings and what God truly desires; the same word is used in the book of Psalms 72:8, 12–14. This is originally a psalm of King Solomon's reign, and his dominion was from sea to sea and from the river to the end of the earth; all nations served Him. However, this was the type of king he was supposed to be according to verse 12–14. He was to deliver the poor and the needy when they called or cried out for help. The dominant king was to have pity on the weak and the less fortunate and was to save the lives of the poor and needy from oppression, mistreatment, and violence. The ruling king would see their lives as precious to God. This is the kind of king God wants in Ezekiel 24:4, one who strengthened the weak, healed the sick, and bound up the injured. Dominion is to do good; that's what the blessing was for: to be like our creator—a benefit, an asset, an advocate to restore, to protect the defenseless, and give justice to the disenfranchised people of this world.

The command was for humanity to exercise dominion over all of creation. You can see that while we are ruling over creation, we are also called to protect it as the kings we are, accepting tribute taxes and tithes from the subordinates to receive a bountiful sustenance from the fruits of creation, yet also as kings, we should take care of the weak and poor of his kingdom, so we are called to guard natural beauty and preserve endangered species of God's creation. Rule with force and even harshness the enemy.

It has been said among the Lord God's radical street soldiers and I concur that the first book of the Bible, Genesis, is the alpha and the omega of the whole Bible and that it summarizes and contains the entire human's scenario. From Eden to the promised land to man's responsibility and his relationship with the Creator to the woman and her input to their disobediences on into the fall. To their dysfunctional children and the infiltration of sin into the human family. The failure to adhere to God's designed purpose created and presented a catastrophic problem that mandated that we have a mediator, so the story ends as it began and it continued. First Timothy 2:5 says, "For there is one God and one mediator between God and man, the Man Christ, the anointed king of Glory Jesus." Hebrews 8:6 But now, He has obtained a more excellent ministry, inasmuch as He (Jesus) is also Mediator of a better covenant, which was established on better promises. All this is accomplished by the Lord Jesus Christ; the death of Christ was necessary for the establishment of the new and better covenant. The stratagem to get man and his kind back into God's good graces would take a tremendous sacrifice of Jesus's dominion and subduing Himself to the cross of Calvary, so the plot and the plan thickens. If you were to look closely after a prayerful talk with the Author of life and then read and examine His holy love letters, you will discover the precious hallowed Spirit prevailing and permeating in our hearts and continuing to open up our mind's eye by the revealing of the mysteries of Godliness. The things that have been concealed from the foundation of the world, the true issues of life, are the discovered treasures. The book of Revelation brings to us full circle right back to the book of Genesis. The journey of man and our kind begins with operating in our God-given identity and in our inheritance as the children of the invisible God and Father with our intrinsic and innate charter as His.

This is an awesome truth to me that the word of God is so resounding and perpetual and how the word of God echoes through time and eternity ringing true the declaration that man and his kind is made in the very image and likeness of God the Father. Yes, the very image of the God the Father the Master of the universe, the Lord of Hosts! So from the very beginning of time and the very essence of man was to have this treasure in an earthen vessel and the treasure is the dominion of knowledge and power of the Holy Ghost imparted in us. This dominion God has given to us over the earth and all the animals and creatures. Just to interject for a moment this fascinating point God has in the book of Jeremiah chapter 27: how God tells the king of Babylon, Nebuchadnezzar, that he has been given power and dominion over the beasts of the field and the nations of the earth. Yes, God can and will ordain whomsoever He will and please. A man—mind you, a heathen man, a pagan, a bad man, and a proud man—as a servant of the Most High God. What a wonderful epiphany! What say you, revelation?

Let's examine Romans 9:17, "So then it is not of him who wills nor of him who runs, but of God who shows mercy; for the scripture says to the Pharaoh, for this very purpose I have raised you up, is that I may show My power in you and that My name be declared in all the earth." Paul makes it clear: God is free to employ instruments which oppose His purpose but will lead to his ultimate goal and glory through opposition and persecution has only served to promote God's end.

In the book of Romans 9:20–22, it goes on to say, "For indeed O man who, are you to reply against God? Will the thing formed say to him who formed it, why have you made me like this? Does not the potter have power over the clay, from the same lump to make one vessel for honor and another for dishonor? Question; can God be sovereign and the divine creator of the lump of humanity or does he need to ask man's permission? What if God wanted to show His wrath and to make His power known, endured with much long suffering the vessels of wrath prepared for destruction, and he might make known the riches of His glory on the vessels of mercy which He had prepared beforehand for glory."

In addition, if you have not noticed yet, God can and will do what He will with His creation and to those who will question God's rights of His action is incongruous. Creation has no right to object to what their Creator does. However, God exercises His sovereignty in abundant mercy and not just in strict justice. God's mercy is still evident to the world as he engrafted the Gentiles and all non-Jewish people into his plan of salvation and adopted family.

If God would do this to a pagan man and nation, certainly, He will and can do it with his children, but we must know and understand that our Father most definitely wants us to operate in our God-given dominion and subduing power over the earth and these earthen vessels. This is the revelation that will awaken and transform us from a mere mundane human being into an increasable God-fearing believer with the knowledge that Christ is in us, the hope of glory. We have become partakers of the Godhead bodily in Christ where we move, live, and have our being; we as men and women of God are made to mimic to imitate and to copy our big brother, Almighty Jesus the Christ, by possessing the knowledge of the kingdom that is in heaven, God's throne. The Lord God have given man and his kind the pinnacle position as His masterpiece in all of creation that we may have dominion and power to control, discipline, and to tame the earth. Man has supreme authority and power to reign, to rule, and to prevail over our own animated clay bodies. Just like the allegory Pinocchio had to come to grips with his sinful nature by stop lying and to control his nature to become a human being, so do we to become true children of God in a God-given and a God-ordained environment. The house of prayer and praise, the church, which is his own kingdom on earth. God conditionally offered the kingdom to Adam and Eve to have dominion and to subdue it, but they fell to restrain themselves and keep things in check. So ever since the fall of man (Adam and Eve), the earth has become the stage of global and universal rebellion against God.

Luke 4:5–6 illustrates the temptation narrative: "Then the devil, taking Jesus up on a high mountain, showed Him all the kingdoms of the world in a moment of time. And the devil said to Him, 'All this authority I will give You, and their glory, for this has been delivered to me, and I give it to whomever I wish.'" The temptation of Jesus solicits a compelling messianic proof rather than earthly power. Jesus affirms exclusive worship of God the Father, and Jesus Christ humbly obeyed and suffered as planned. For this purpose and reason, the son of God was manifest that he might destroy the works of the devil.

First John 5:19–20 says, "We know that we are of God, and the whole world lies under the sway of the wicked one. And we know that the Son of God has come and has given us an understanding, that we may know Him who is true; and we are in Him who is true, in His Son Jesus Christ. This is the true God and eternal life." These two scriptures identify and distinguish between the two rulers: one rules the earth and the other rules the world. As children of God, we are commissioned to rule the earth and all that's in it, on it, and beneath it and our hemisphere. We must control our earth self. The word of God tells us that the "earth is the Lord's and all its fullness the world and those who dwell therein" (Psalm 24:1–2). However, Satan has been given control of the world through lust and through pride; the flesh, which is this man, made a sophisticated system of culture, religion, economics as of now. Satan has influenced the world to drink of his wine of delusion and intoxication to think and act out of the norm out of their righteous mind, their sober mind, and their Christ mind. Yet God has not given us the spirit of fear, of phobias, by respecting, honoring, or reverencing anything but Him. But He has given us power—the ability to love and become compassionate with a sober and sound mind—the very mind of Christ Jesus to subdue and take dominion in love and an abstemious mind to love the hell out of everyone we come into contact with. Israel however should have been our example through Abraham, Isaac, and Jacob and was shown favor that they should be to God a kingdom of priests (Exodus 19:6). The entire nation was to fulfill the priestly duty of worship and service to the Lord God the Father; however, Israel's failure to fulfill God's covenant resulted in the selection of the next phase: the covenant of the Aaronic priesthood. That also fell short of God's glory; this now brings in the new and better covenant of grace. Grace has constituted all believers a spiritual kingdom, a holy and royal priesthood (1 Peter 2:5–9). Israel, however, through declaring still a nominal allegiance shared in the same common rebellion as the rest of the world and after Israel had rejected the Son of God, they were then casted away. Henceforth was not permanently broken off;

but only for a season until a complete number of gentiles came to God (Romans 11:15, 20:25). So now, the kingdom of God is calling upon all men everywhere without distinction of race or nationality to submit voluntarily to God's rule, and His rule is when it is acknowledged by whoever will. For God had relinquished His sovereignty in the face of rebellion but declared by promise to establish it.

Meanwhile, God is seeking a willing, obedient servant (i.e., slave). God gives His laws to a nation and appoints those who truly believe to be a royal and holy priestly people, to administrate His kingdom, that is to have dominion, which is government that does not come into the range of the natural powers of observation (Luke 17:20–21) but is within you, spiritually discerned. Dominion helps describe the nature we are naturally made in God's image and likeness. Knowing now God is obviously a spirit, He did not exactly create us like himself in appearance, but again, He did. Although God the Father did not have a physical body, but His Word did. His Word became flesh, and we beheld him as the only begotten Son full of grace and truth. God the Son, Jesus Christ, is the fullness of the Godhead bodily (Colossians 2:2–10). God, for His full countenance of divine nature, lives in Christ's humanity. Moreover, we have full life in union with Christ Jesus, for Christ has supreme rule and authority over all things. Jesus is the Word of God that became flesh; furthermore, we are a reflection of God's glory, for Christ is in you, the hope of glory and love. We have put on the new man, resembling the Godhead bodily, that is in our bodies. We are to mimic the Godhead bodily: to imitate and emulate Jesus' works. We are to live like the Godhead bodily: to talk like the Godhead in our bodies, and even to look like the Godhead in our bodies.

You say we are to what? That's right: mimic to live, to talk, and even to look like the Godhead in our bodies, and I say yes, for sure, listen to this. However, it is nothing we can do on our own but believe the unadulterated word of God, without mixture, tradition, philosophy, and rudiments of this world and Satan, which is renewed in knowledge, after the image of Him who created us. You know we can live like the Godhead bodily, and this is how the word of God tells us in the book of Leviticus 20:7, 12:45 to sanctify ourselves and be holy for God is holy. This is God's way and will for our lives. We must know the power and the ability we have in Christ, the same capability to speak like God in our humanity and to call those things that are not as though they were. We are also to understand that the word of faith is even in our mouth, for the word is powerful and a creative force. The power of death and life is in the tongue. We can create things, we can heal the sick and brokenhearted, or we can kill and destroy a man's spirit and dreams with our words and speech, believing humanity needs to look like the Godhead bodily, to reflect the greater light, by letting our light shine so that men might see our good works and give the Lord God our Father all the glory that is so rightly His.

To subdue is to bring all things under control by influence, by training, by persuasion, and/or by force.

Verse 26 says, "Then God said, 'Let Us make man in Our image, according to Our likeness; let them have dominion over the fish of the sea, over the birds of the air, and over the cattle, over all the earth and over every creeping thing that creep on the earth." This was an awesome event of creation that happened on the sixth day: the higher level man and his kind was made. The element in the creation of man was that he was to be in the image and the likeness of the Godhead bodily, and this plural references to the Triune God/Trinity. "Let_us make man in *our* image and *our* likeness" indicates a special decision, presented as if it was made at some great assembly and the gravity of the decision stresses that something new was about to occur. The plural phrase "let *us*" and *our* also suggests the community of the Godhead, which involves three persons: God the Father, God the Son, and God the Holy Ghost coming together in agreement. The theologian Leopold argues for the Christian faith that this resemblance would show itself above all in our dominion over the animal kingdom and over all the earth. We have been given the ability, the power, and the will over every living creature that moves on the face of the earth. We are able to talk, dialogue, understand, reason, and even work together with animals of all kinds. Dogs we train and win our hearts, cats steal our fancy, birds capture our imaginations, and fish of all sorts—dolphins, sharks, and octopus—encourage us to dive into deep waters to swim like them. Cattle and horses we have domesticated. In the immediate context, it showed itself in our ability to have communion with God; ultimately, and perhaps most important of all, it made the incarnation of the Word of God certainly possible in Emmanuel. This was to cause Eden-like conditions throughout the earth. Complete conformity to God's plan is what man and his kind was commissioned to do.

Subdue (*kabas*) literally means to "stamp out or on" something or somebody and to rule over (*radah*), literally "tread down" negative situations like fear and doubt. God told Jeremiah in 1:10, "See I have this day set you over the nations and over the kingdom, to root out and to pull down to root out and to pull down, to destroy and to throw down, to build and to plant." This shows that God was presenting man and woman with a major task. We were blessed by God and assigned a twofold ministry: simply to increase and to multiply in number and fill the earth with like-minded persons as offspring. This was a gift from God, not a burden. We were to occupy and enjoy God's creation, not fear it. This is also a way we could serve and glorify our God and Maker by caring for His creation. We should be able to recognize the God in every man and every woman we see all around us or nowadays realize the anti-spirit in them. We know that we should not worship any animals or anything on earth or under the earth according to these scriptures (Exodus 20:4; Roman 1:21–23). Behold the affliction to any person who lowers himself/herself to the level of animals by giving an animal or an image of an animal the place that belongs only to God alone. God also created both our bodies and our spirit, and we must not artificially separate the two and think that we can ignore our bodies while living to God in our spirit. The scripture makes it perfectly clear that we must not mistreat our own bodies or those of others we are to glorify God in our body and in our spirit, said 1 Corinthians 6:19–20. It is very important to note that we were permitted to rule only over other living creatures, not over other human beings. Nowhere in scripture is men given authority to dominate the woman or vice versa, neither our fellow man that bears the image of the Creator, and we are not to be dominated but to be ministered to.

So let them have dominion, let them command, and have say-so. Man was made to dominate their own personal space but not one another's.

Let talk about all four of these ingredients that make up this phenomenon called subjugation, the art of concurring.

> So God created man in his own image, in the image of God created he him; male and female created he them. And God blessed them, and God said unto them, "Be fruitful, and multiply, and replenish the earth, and subdue it: and have dominion over the fish of the sea, and the fowl/ birds of the air, and over every living thing that moveth upon the earth."

So from the very existence of man, God has commanded Adam and Eve—man's nativity and their future descendants—we are to subdue and have dominion over the earth and all of its animals and creatures, the world, their own flesh, and the body. So let's examine the word *subdue*, which is a fascinating facade for there are at least six words to define.

Subdue, five words are in the Hebrew tongue and one is in the Greek. These are the Hebrew words with great expressions. *Dawbar* [#1696] is to arrange, to speak rarely in a destructive sense, to answer, appoint, command, and to declare. As our Creator, so too is ours to call those things that are not as though they were *dawbar*, the words of our mouth and the meditation of our hearts spoken and came to pass; death and life in the power of our tongue, for our tongues are a created force—the apparatus for proclaiming, pronouncing, and affirming God's word. Consequently, we have been employed, selected, and appointed by the Lord God Almighty, chosen as His inheritance.

Then there is *kaw-bash* [#3533] described as to tread down, to disregard negatively, to conquer, and to subjugate. The third definition is *kaw-nah* [#3665]. It is to bend the knee in humiliation and to vanquish. The forth definition is *radad*, pronounced "raw-dad"

[#7288]: to tread in pieces, to conquer, and to overlay by spreading. *Saphal* is the fifth word, sounded out "shaw-fale" [#8214]; its meaning is to depress or to sink in humility, to abase, to cast, and put down debase. The sixth word is the Greek equivalent *hoop-st-as-so* [#5293], which simply means under, beneath, subordinate, and obedience.

We subdue things that demand submission and humiliation, which is a powerful form of discipline. The word *subdue* is used most of the time in a negative and destructive way in its content dealing with the world and its scheme, rudiments, teachings, thoughts, ideas, and suggestions. The world is another kingdom with an anti–Jesus Christ and Godhead-ship. Whatever the world says or suggests, consider it absolutely wrong and false! This is what we as Christians are fighting over and for what God the Father commands and what the world and Satan suggest. Our job as the stewards and ordained occupants of this planet called earth is that we must *hoopstasso* the world and its influence unto us the church of God in Christ. However, it is a positive, bold, and radical word in their original conception. Its meaning is to bend thy knee, to bow down low, and to tread down the weakness of the flesh. So you can see the word of God tells Adam and Eve and us today to base these earthen vessels and to master our human nature, to bring it down, to bring it into subjection, to be subordinate, to be obedient, to bring into bondage, and to conquer the earth. I say the flesh, you know the body, the dust of the ground. We have been given the privilege to subdue it and to bring things under control. We are ordered to multiply and fill the earth with our offspring and to subdue it by godly influence, godly training, godly persuasion, and in some exception, by force. We also have been told to master our atmosphere by taking dominion over all animals; that includes all birds and all fish and creatures of the ocean.

So let us unscramble the marred facts of a subdued life. We first need to understand how the word *influence* operates in getting folks to become subordinate; it is the power over men or things by affecting the mind of mankind, swaying them to believe and concur with the greater/supreme authority of God. Influencing us through his love in Jesus Christ our Lord, that wonderful word of love, the

Lord of all. We, as Christian under the anointing of Christ, must manifest the power to subdue this old wretched world's system by controlling this earthen vessel to respond to the commands of the Father through discipline, instruction, and education. In order to overcome, everyone must have a godly, sanctified Spirit-filled training that provides instruction and discipline as becoming disciples of Jesus Christ God's only begotten Son. Then we have the word *persuasion*. It is to win over by having the power of conviction and of conversion through good advice, good godly rhetoric, and wise counsel that strongly wins one's heart over. Jesus Christ, our anointed King and Lord, is our awesome example of subjugation and meekness—power under control. Jesus, the Christ King, is the greatest conqueror of all time by persuading his enemies to reconcile their hearts by convincing them and us of our misunderstanding of God's loving grace and mercy, also by allowing us to miss the mark, falling short of His glory. Nevertheless, showing His love and commitment to spreading the light in our life, converting us to believe the beautiful truth of the glorious Gospel of the Lord Jesus Christ and that we are sons of the King, and that Entails an heir of God's kingdom. The next word is *force*. This word fills the hearts of most human beings in the world today that would like to subdue others by force and have; however, we must apply pressure to ourselves by producing strength and energy to change, to overpower, to strain, and to compel ourselves as humans to be subdued. We were given dominion and power, but we have failed to use the discipline required to control our own flesh, for if we can subdue ourselves, we can control the earth. So it is imperative to enslave ourselves from ourselves for the spirit and the flesh is at war against each other.

The spirit is willing, but the flesh is weak; the spirit is willing to do what? So glad you asked if the spirit is willing to obey the word and will of the Lord our God and Father. No matter how you perceive it, as long as we are on this mundane shore, there will always be a servant-master relationship going on, whether it is a boss-worker relationship, an employer-employee relationship, or a customer-proprietor relationship. I personally love the waiter-diner relationship. There is always someone ordering and someone serving, somebody in charge and somebody under the charge. The spirit is willing. However, the flesh is weak. I mean weak, weak, weak as water, weak as dirt, weak as a feather, weak as not being able to handle or control anything in meekness; the flesh is just a big, old pushover. We as the people of God must subdue our own individual flesh vessel by bending it down, by bowing it down, by breaking it down, by humiliating it, by enslaving it. In order to be exhaled through Jesus, we must obey the word of God. This is awesome; why would God want us to have dominion over his wonderful creation? Such a high-octane call that man and his kind have received.

God's purpose was and is to establish a physical world that would mimic, copy, and model his spiritual world. A world descending from heaven to earth, for man and his offspring to be God's sovereign agent in the earth governed by the Holy Spirit to subdue and have dominion to reproduce God's kingdom as kings here on earth to rule, reign, and to take authority in meekness. Meekness is an awesome and dynamic attribute that humankind needs to possess to emulate God's will, God's purpose, and God's plan. Meekness is defined and translated as power under extreme control. It is strength and the ability to judge and to discern with the righteousness of God's judgment. Jesus is the ultimate example of meekness. Christ is the expressed image of God that we need to see and copy. Jesus is the Christ, which simply means he's the anointed King of Glory, the King of kings.

In the kingly office of Christ, there are three special relationships that Christ represents. For the people, He is the mediator in the relationship between God and man; He is a prophet, a priest, and a king. These three offices are not three separate offices, but are three offices functioning as one office as Christ the mediator. Christ the King is the preeminent sovereign head over the kingdom of the church of God according to the gospel of Ephesians 1:22, 4:15 and the book of Colossians 1:18. Christ executing his mediator kingship in his ecclesia, the holy nation, and over his church and over all the things in behalf of his church. The kingdom of his power and of his providential government.

Contra-ouler is to have control. To control is to have influence by applying weight and pressure, God created man and his kind through the first Adam to have dominion over the earth by being under God's command by being regulated, checked, and restrained, directed to test the power over one's enemy, but he lost it to Satan the devil. Never to fear, God incarnated himself to be his only begotten son, the second Adam—I mean the last Adam—Jesus of Nazareth to regain order and control. So in the book of Genesis 1:27, God created human beings to be like his son, the incarnated one, and he made them male and female, and God blessed them and said, "Have many children so that your descendants will live all over the earth." To bring it under control, saying, "I will put you in charge of the fish of the sea, the birds of the air, and all the wild animals." The commandment is from the Lord God, *sawah* [#6680]. Essentially, this verb refers to a verbal communication by which a superior "orders" or "commands" to a subordinate to do something. The word implies the content of what was said. God ordered and commanded Pharaoh to let his people go, and Pharaoh let the children of Israel go so that they could worship Yahweh their Lord God, and Pharaoh sent them away with great provisions. This order defines an action relevant to a specific situation: *sawah* can also denote command in the sense of the establishment of a rule by which a subordinate is to act in every recurring similar situation. In the book of Genesis 2:16, the first appearance of the word *sawah* in the Bible is when God commanded Adam in the Garden of Eden. God set down the law and rules: "Of every tree of the garden thou may eat freely; but the tree in the midst of the garden of good and evil: you must not eat of the fruit of that tree or you will surely die." When commanded to heed the order, one must carry out and accomplish the order of a superior. It means to commission a charge such as the act of commanding, telling, and even sending someone to do a particular task. The most frequent subject of this verb is God himself; however, God is not to be questioned or commanded to be explained. The work of his hand in the book of Isaiah 45:11 shows us that God's commands are unique and that they require an inner commitment and not just an external obedience as he commands men to do.

Miswah God is always the giver of the Law, the *miswah* saying, "All the commandments which I command you ye shall observe to do that you may live." The plural of *miswah* often denotes a body of laws given by divine revelation; they are the words of God. Outside the Pentateuch, commandments are given by the king's orders. *Prostagma* is an injunction meaning subordination or discipline. Control also is to influence by weight and/or pressure. God created man-Adam and his kind and the second Adam, Jesus the Christ, and his kind, his disciplined disciples, to influence his kingdom dominion decision and to be God's agent by ruling and subduing the rest of earth and creation, including the crafty forces of Satan. God's sovereignty is the necessary beginning point of our study. The theme is the kingdom of God. As the Bible opens here, we meet the King of Glory, universal sovereign whose realm, reign, and regency are described at the outset. His realm is the scope of his rule. The transcending power not only includes the spiritual world, but also the entire physical universe, which it exceeds. God existed before all creation. He expands beyond it, and by virtue of having begotten it, God Yehovah encompasses all that it is. He reigns by the power which he rules is exercised through his will, his way, and his words. By His own will, God the Father creatively decides and designs; by His own word, He speaks creation into being; and by His own works, His spirit displays His unlimited power. God's regency and His authority to rule are in His preexistence and His holiness. God was there before creation in the beginning. Thus, as its creator, He deserves to be its potentate. His benevolent intent in creating all things well reveals His holy nature that is complete and perfect, and thus, His moral right to be creation's King for all kingdom, power, and authority flows from Him, God Yehovah. The book of 1 John tells us the whole world lieth in wickedness under Satan's power; and Satan and his world and this earth will be destroyed by the power of God, and God will establish his kingdom in the new heaven and the new earth for them. Jesus would have put down all principalities and powers under his feet by breaking them to pieces and consuming all other nation and kingdoms for Jesus must reign. Daniel 2:44–47, 7:14 speaks of the God of heaven; permanent existence distinguishes it from all its previous ones and Daniel's vision of the throne of the Ancient of Days over-ruling all others. Then there's the Son of Man who is none other than the Lord Jesus Himself, our Messiah, the anointed King of Glory. The kingdom of God and the kingdom of heaven, for at time, they are identical but cannot be used indiscriminately, for the kingdom of God is a moral kingdom in its broader aspect. The entire sphere is under God's rule where the second Adam—Jesus our Lord—the inheritance of God the Father where man has dominion. However, the kingdom of heaven is God's domain, dispensational and a distinguished place like the earth; nevertheless, the action that is related to the world of God is in heaven. Psalm 22:28, 145:13 is an antithesis to man and his world. God in heaven totally, unequivocally opposes, contrasts. In other words, God don't want what man is working with and man really doesn't want what God is working with. We want power, but we don't want to subdue ourselves. A man with power would try to control others and subdue someone else but can't come within ten feet of getting control and subduing ourselves in discipline and in love (Daniel 4:25; Luke 1:25; Romans 13:1).

In the pages of Daniel's book chapter 4, it shows how God the Father orchestrated his marvelous works to allow man to have dominion but also to recognize the author and sovereign of all power and authority. As God did unto the king of Babylon, Nebuchadnezzar: God of the universe spoke to Nebuchadnezzar in a dream. The second time as he rested and was flourishing in his palace. He spoke, saying, "Look what I have done with my mighty power and my honor of my majesty!" While the word was still in the king's mouth, the voice from heaven came down, and the Lord God spoke to the king of Babylon, saying, "The kingdom has been stripped from your hands. And you shall be driven from men and eat grass like a beast of the field for seven years."

Although Nebuchadnezzar has seen the miraculous work of the Lord God and believed the power that gave Daniel the power to interpret his dream, but the king's heart was still filled with pride—pride the monster. Pride is the thing that keeps us out of the will and the kingdom of God. However, God still shows his merciful attitude toward arrogant persons like King Nebuchadnezzar, as well as God's desire is that the world powers surrender control to His Lordship.

> And the twenty-four elders and the four living creatures fell down and worshiped God who sat on the throne, saying, "Amen! Alleluia!" Then a voice came from the throne, saying "Praise our God, all you His Servants and those who fear Him, both small and great!" (Revelation 19:4–5)

To the only wise God our Savior, in the name of the Lord Jesus Christ of Nazareth, we fall down in awe of Thee, it is my prayer to honor and worship you in total submission and dominion as Thy servant of the Most High God. Alleluia, alleluia, and amen!

CHAPTER 3

The Law Concerning Slavery
Leviticus 25:39–55

God truly ordained slavery and has established a law concerning it because slavery is ubiquitous, for it is everywhere in the world and has been in society throughout all dispensations from the past, to this present time, and on into the future may be under a different heading, but the effects and position are the same. The effects are services, work, labor, production; however, the position is to do it all in the spirit of loving humility. Slavery will always exist as long as there are human bodies of flesh and blood for the body and bodies personify a slave and slavery, for you can't have slaves without bodies nor bodies without slaves—they are synonymous. So we endure the adversities and the struggle of transitioning these earthen vessels into becoming sons. The inheritance of the king knowing that a son is treated as a servant until our Lord Jesus Christ of Nazareth comes back. Therefore we must understand that every government, every kingdom, and every principality are appointed, established, and ordained of God. For they are a reflection of God and his kingdom in heaven, for the concept has to do with order. For we know that the Roman government was the first century and only kingdom to become the human prototype of God's kingdom on earth.

The Romans set up branches of governments: executive, legislative, and judicial had the order and laws. As the kingdom of

God, they conquered and subjugated nations and established their government right there in the foreign land and went out, permeating the world through colonization and establishment with their brand of thinking, with their laws, with their rules, with their ways, with their standards, and with their king. God sets things in order, God the Father executive; God the Son legislature writes the law and gives the word of the Father; and the Holy Spirit, the judge, judging in righteousness. The kingdom of God and the Romans' kingdom ranking things in order for position, ordering a change of command. God desiring his people to know the levels of servants, stages of services, and degrees of ministry. The law of slavery was grafted for the children of Israel under Moses in the books of Exodus 21:1–8 and Leviticus 25:39–55, as well as Deuteronomy 15:12–18. The percept was to enable the poor of the land to excess by getting them out of debt. Debt—what a monster of a master; under the Indentured Slavery Act, slavery was also to show humiliation so the people would look to God for provision because God is the supplier of all our needs according to his riches in glory through Christ Jesus. Humiliation shows our need and reverence to God as all powerful and the provider of our needs. The laws of slavery were also used to humbly submit a people or an entire nation that was living in pride and arrogance or just evil. The law of slavery reveals to us that we can't do whatever we desire and think we are big enough to do and for us to know that God the Father alone is sovereign, the Lord and Master of the universe.

Topic—the law of slavery and the release: permanent slaves could be acquired by purchase or as prisoners of war. They were to be taken only from the nation and people outside Canaan (Leviticus 25:39–55). Verse 42 tells us that the people of Israel are the Lord's slaves and have been brought out of Egypt and must not be sold into slavery and treated harshly, but if they needed slaves, they could buy them from other nations around them as well as buy the children of the foreigners who are living among them. Their foreign children born in the land may become your property and you can leave them as an inheritance to your children whom they must serve as long as they live, but you must not treat any Israelites harshly, and if a foreigner living with them become rich while some Israelites become poor and sell themselves as a slaves to that foreigner or to a member of that foreigner's family, after they are sold, they still have the right to be bought back by a brother or an uncle. Even a cousin or any close relative may be able to buy them back. Or if they themselves earn enough money or time, they may buy their own freedom. They must consult the one who bought them, and they must count the years from the time they sold themselves until the next year of jubilee or the restoration and must set the price for their release on the basis of the wages paid the hired workers. They must refund a part of the purchase price according to the number of years left as if they had been hired on a normal basis. Their master must not treat them harshly, and if they are not set free in any of these ways, they and their children must be set free in the next year of jubilee (i.e., the restoration of Israelites). The Jewish people cannot be permanent slaves because the people of Israel are the Lord God's very own slaves. God had brought and bought them out of Egypt. He is their Lord and God, but permanent slaves were considered permanent members of their master household.

> And the Lord said unto Moses and Aaron, "This is the ordinance of the Passover: there shall no stranger eat there of: but every man's slave-servant that is bought for money, when thou hast circumcised him, then shall he eat thereof. They were circumcised and admitted to the Passover and all the special festivals and sacrifices except the quilt offering. Slaves could be forced to work, but if they were beaten severely, they were to be set free." (Exodus 12:43–44)

> If a slave was killed, their master was punished. God has ordinance for provision also as fugitive slaves were not to be returned to their owners or treated as slaves. Owners were forced to treat their slaves humanely. (Exodus 21:20–21)

Thou shall not deliver unto his master the servant which is escaped from his master unto thee; he shall dwell with thee even among you, in that place which he shall choose in one of thy gates, where it liketh him best thou shalt not oppress him. (Deuteronomy 23:15–16)

The Treatment of Slaves

If any Israelite, male or female, sell themselves to you as a slave you art to release them after they have served you for six years when the seventh year comes you must let them go free, but when you set them free, don't send them away empty handed give to them generously from what the Lord has blessed you with how be it sheep, goat, grain, or wine. Remember that you were once slaves in Egypt and the Lord your God set you free; that is why I am now giving you this command. (Deuteronomy 15:12–18)

You may have, at this time, gleaned from these pages that God had intended for Israel's form of slavery was for the means of economy's welfare for a time to recover an opportunity for the poor to be supported the same way in today's time. We use chapter 8 or 11 bankruptcy and unemployment to get back on your feet; this, as well, is a form of indentured servitude. However, some slaves may not want to leave their good masters and families because they have come to love them and have became content to stay with them.

So the master took his servant to the door of the temple house and there pierced his ears; a symbol of a permanent enslavement he will then be the master slave for life. Treat your female slave in the same manner and don't be resentful when you set your slaves free; after all they have served you well for six years at half the cost of a hired servant. Do this and the Lord your God will bless you in all that you do. (Exodus 21:6–8)

The symbol of a permanent slave or a prisoner is the piercing of the ears. In our society today, piercings are the rave and a serious fad for men and women. Man and his kind have enslaving themselves to masters that don't care much about them and their welfare—selfish, greedy, and wicked. There are many masters, but there is only one true and benevolent master and lord, Jesus the Christ, the lover of our soul. Glory to God the Father!

I remember when I was about twenty-six, going on twenty-seven in the month of August 1987, I had been desiring and wanted to get my ears pierced for some time, but never had the nerves to go through with it. Then one day that summer, at an African world festival in downtown Detroit, Michigan, where I made a *doulos'* decision to enslave myself to a world of vanity and foolishness. I was a young saved married man at the time, and I love the Lord God and believed in the Lord Jesus Christ as my personal savior; nevertheless, I lusted for an image of my own reputation to follow, just like a messed-up Nimrod. On that evening of the festival, my wife was not with me. If she had been, she would not have agreed with my decision. As I perused through the crowd and viewed the festivities, I came to a booth where there was a beautiful black woman, statuesque as an African queen, and she was advertising earrings and piercings and she said these words that drew me to finally getting my ear pierced. She said, "Every king should have them!"

Not knowing that I was already a king and the son of the King of kings. Nevertheless, there it was. I became compelled to have my ears pierced, and this began the height of my vainness, simple vainglory, the vanity of vanities, and my proud marine-cropped arrogant, selfish self. I became a slave to emptiness, vanity, and vainglory. A narcissistic, self-evolved, self-absorbed person. Not understanding the severity of the drastic decision I've made; thanks be to God for the victory through our Lord and Savior Jesus Christ for His amazing grace and His atoning blood. For He called me his own; I was brought with a price and ordained as a minister and a disciple of Jesus the Christ my King. This brought me to the morning several months after I got my ears pierced when I woke up from sleep and slumber, and my earring was out of my ear. So I tried to put it back into my ear, but they would not go back in. I then tried again and again, but the earrings wouldn't go back in. In one day overnight, my ear was closed shut completely. I just could not believe that my ear was closed shut, so I became emphatic and asked my wife to help me push the earring in as hard as she could, and my ear started to bleed, so I never was able to wear my earring anymore. I truly believe God closed my ear in retrospect; a week before my ear closed, my pastor at the time, the late reverent Dr. William Holly of the New Rising Star MBC called me to become a deacon in the church of God. A servant, a minister, and a slave in love reconciliation, all the while I have been feeling the burden of his acceptable services; therefore, I said, "Lord, I yield! I yield! To God be the glory!"

There is a correlation between the husband and wife relationship, between God and mankind's relationship, between parents and children relationship, and between master and slave relationship, and it is the thread of love that runs through all these relationships in honor, obedience, surrender, and humility.

CONTINUAL THOUGHT:

> For you are all sons of God through faith in Christ Jesus. For as many of you as were baptized into Christ have put on Christ. There is neither Jew nor Greek, there is neither slave nor free, there is neither male nor female; for you are all one in Christ Jesus. and if you are Christ's then you are Abraham's seed, and heirs according to the promise. (Galatians 3:26–29)

There are many divers of manifestations of faith in Christ, but it is faith in Christ that creates unity and harmony. The act of obedience in Christ Jesus through baptism is to put on Christ as a new garment and covering. Through Christ Jesus, the old racial schism and divisions have been bound and healed, like the notorious social strife and conflict of classes; the ethnic divide of Jews and gentiles, and the gender wars of males and females. God wants social harmony, unity, and equity among one another—no distinction. We are family in the body of Christ

> Now I say that the heir, as long as he is a child, does not differ at all from a slave, though he is master of all, but is under guardians and steward until the time appointed by the father. Even so we, when we were children, were in bondage under the elements of the world. But when the fullness of time had come, God sent forth His Son, born of a woman, born under the law, to redeem those who were under the law, so that we might receive the adoption as sons.
>
> And because you are sons, God has sent forth the Spirit of His Son into your hearts, crying out "Abba, Father!" Therefore you are no longer a slave but a son, and if a son, then an heir of God through Christ Jesus. (Galatians 4:1–7)

Paul paints a picture of a concept of the inheritance of the covenant promise. God appointed the law as a kind of guardian or custodian to discipline and restrain us, mankind, until the coming of the Savior, the Lord Jesus Christ. Although the minor in the illustration is a rightful heir (he is also underage and under the school master's supervision), he is treated no different from a slave in the sense that he is unable to make significant decisions for himself. Freedom as a son, when the fullness of time comes—the time fixed and appointed by His Father, a date set by our heavenly Father, the right time determined by God in His inscrutable and infinite wisdom. Then God sent forth His Son as a divine being, Emmanuel, born of a woman and asserting His full humanity. He was born under the law of slavery, the law that also suggested a birthplace providentially arranged, so he might learn sympathy toward sinners and those in bondage.

For Christ Jesus came to redeem those under the law of sin and death by paying the ultimate price, buying us out of sin's curse of bondage. No longer slaves, we are free; we are sons and joint heirs with Christ by God's own act of grace, given to us freely. Access is given to all who believe the promise of *joy* in the Holy Ghost. Amen!

Premeditate, before, accomplish, serve, bring forth, bestow, to appoint, addict, set fulfill, to arrange, in an orderly manner, to assign, or dispose, to ascertain position, or let ordained. God has ordained the masters and the slave; marriage, the husband and wife. God has ordained the family and the children all are connected to God to do and perform the same way. A slave did not ever have to wake up on his own or find work for himself or buy his own food or choose his own transportation. A slave never had to worry about a house or pay his own way; a slave did not have to go to school on his own. He had a schoolmaster, alleluia, and was sent to school to learn the ways of the master. Just listening to his master's words, the master would encourage us that He would supply all our needs according to his riches in glory through Christ Jesus. Wonderful Lord! If we were to read the book of Philippians 4:19, you will discover "that our God shall supply all you need according to his riches in glory by Christ Jesus." The king of the kingdom also supplies all the needs of his subject of the kingdom with protection, provision, and providence. The master, lord, and king has the responsibility for making work for his slave (i.e., servant), and eventually, the servant-master relationship begins to flourish with love and become reciprocal.

The law concerning slavery by humility and the fear of the Lord, Proverbs 22:4, "The reward of humility and reverent fear and respect along with worship and service to the LORD JEHOVAH is riches, honor, and long life." Father God, in the name of Jesus Christ, our Lord and Savior, we give you all the glory and praise. Thank you for your love (i.e.) mercy and grace; your riches (i.e.) peace and joy; and humility (i.e.) power and wisdom. Amen."

CHAPTER 4

Order to Serve
Jeremiah 27

Jeremiah, the prophet, began his ministry in Judah under the reign of the good king Josiah, then under his sons: Jehoahaz, Jehoiakim, Johanan, and Zedekiah; Josiah who temporarily delayed God's promised judgment through reform, by the reemergence of the scripture by reading the word of God, which also included destroying the pagan idols in high places all within Judah and in Samaria. Jeremiah prophesied between 626 BC and shortly after the fall of Jerusalem in 586 BC—sixty-plus years of service. Jeremiah continued to speak and warn the people of Judah and their kings of God's plan for them, but they heeded not to the word of Jeremiah. King Jehoiakim was openly rebellious and hostile to Jeremiah, and the king began to destroy one of the scrolls sent to him by Jeremiah by cutting off a few columns of the scroll at a time and throwing them into the fire. King Jehoiakim, with all his mighty men and the princes, heard the word of Urijah the prophet, who prophesied in the name of the Lord. According to all the words the Lord God gave to Jeremiah, the King Jehoiakim heard the words of Urijah and sought to put him to death, but Urijah fled and went to Egypt. However, the king sent men to Egypt, and they brought Urijah back, and the king killed Urijah the prophet with the sword and cast his body into the graves of the common people.

King Zedekiah seceded Jehoiakim, and he had issues of his own, for he was a weak and a double-minded king, vacillating between right and wrong and, at times, seeking the advice of Jeremiah 27:1–6 and, at other times, the advice of his enemies, allowing them to misuse, mistreat, and imprison Jeremiah. So now, God commanded Jeremiah to go stand in the house of the Lord and not diminish, shun, or avoid to declare a word that the Lord of Hosts will make the house of Israel and the city of Jerusalem a curse and like the destroyed temple in Shiloh. Shiloh was a city in Ephraim about thirty-five miles north of Jerusalem. This site was chosen for the erection of the tabernacle for its central location, for the Ark of the Covenant was there for more than one hundred years according to the word recorded in the book of Joshua chapter 18. Hopefully, everyone will listen and take heed; however, the people became angry and threatened to murder Jeremiah. However, sober minds prevailed, and Jeremiah escaped death. Jeremiah continued to speak the oracles of God against Judah and Jerusalem and now including the foreign nation to submit to the symbol of service with the bond and yokes God has ordered.

> In the beginning of the reign of Jehoiakim the son of Josiah king of Judah came this word unto Jeremiah from the Lord; saying. Thus saith the Lord to me; make three bonds and yokes, and put them upon thy neck. And send them to the King of Edom, and to the King of Moab, and to the King of the Ammonites, and to the king of Tyrus, and to the king of Zidon, by the hand of the messenger which come to Jerusalem unto Zedekiah king of Judah; And command them to say unto their masters. Thus saith the Lord of Hosts the God of Israel; Thus shall ye say unto your masters; I have made the earth, the man, and the beast that are upon the ground, by my great power and by my outstretched arm, and have given it unto whom it seemed meet unto me. Now have I given all these lands into the

hand of Nebuchadnezzar the king of Babylon, My servant; (All is made and made to serve God the good and the bad) and the beast of the field have I given him also to serve him. So all nations shall serve him and his sons and his son's son, until the time of his land comes; and then many nations and great king shall make him serve them And it shall be, that the nation and kingdom which will not serve Nebuchadnezzar the king of Babylon, and which will not put its neck under the yoke of the political system of the king of Babylon, God is manipulating Babylon as his conduit to colonized the world one section at a time by first getting these nations to submit to the King of Babylon without war being wedged were murder and mayhem would be everywhere; so to keep them from being uprooted and dislocated God the father appointed a political submission to all nation, but the nation that will not listen and obey I will punish, says the Lord, with the sword, the famine and the pestilence, until I have consumed them by his hand.

To be a disobedient or a bad steward/slave caused for some serious disciplinary action; seventy years and three generations of rulers were promised by God, then the end came to Babylon, but before the doom of Babylon, the sword, the famine, and the pestilence to any nation and kingdom that rebelled and would not submit and serve the king of Babylon, Nebuchadnezzar, and put their neck under his yoke.

Jeremiah received the word from the Lord years before he made for himself bonds and yokes and put them on his neck with leather thongs. He first heard this word in the days of Jehoiakim, perhaps around 609 BC, and heard them again during the reign of King Zedekiah, probably around 593 BC, nearly sixteen years later. God ordered Jeremiah and all of humankind to yoke up with Him out of obedience and through submission and humility

The one-trillion-dollar question we need to ask is why would God allow or put people in such a disposition as slavery. In addition, His very own children; better yet, why put them under such a man as King Nebuchadnezzar? A known blasphemer, a known pagan worshiper, a known narcissistic, self-centered, egotistical, pathological, sociopathic, perverted, lascivious known person to lead or become the master and lord over his people Israel and Judah. Simply because the children of Israel and Judah were also operating in these superlatives. Israel and Judah were known for blaspheming, for worshiping pagans, and for being a self-centered people. They were known for their pathological untruths and their prejudiced treatment toward other nations, tribes, and people and for being a nation of sociopaths socially unaccepted. Lascivious and perverted Israel and Judah hated that which they saw in themselves; however, God wanted them to see how it looks to see your sins magnified and photocopied, for when we see others actions resemble yours, you'll tend to abhor them.

This does not suggest that God approves of corrupt and ungodly government officials or unjust legislators; sometimes, however, the Lord God allows evil and bad rulers to punish His people—man and his kind—for a season for instruction and to discipline. God grants authority to serve good ends. Although obedience to earthly authority is the general rule and a clear biblical principle is that we may need to disobey government if commanded to sin or rebel against God. For loyalty to God always trumps any authority against God and takes priority over all human authority. Esther 4:16 and Daniel 3:12–18, 6:10 are good examples of this principle. In Esther chapter 4, Mordecai, her uncle, hears of Haman's plot to extinguish all Jews, so he reaches out to ask for Queen Esther's help! So verse 16 gives us a glimpse of how you might sometimes have to defy laws and authority. Esther conveys to Mordecai to "Go, gather together all the Jews that are present in Shushan, and fast ye for me, and neither eat nor drink three days night and day: I also and my maidens will fast likewise; and so I will go in unto the King, which is not according to the law; and if I perish, then I perish." Sometimes in life, you will have to break some laws to keep the faith; Esther did that and God got the victory to praise the Lord. "Nebuchadnezzar…my servant! And the beasts of the field have I given him also to serve him" (verse 6).

Another story that works the same way is in the book of Daniel 3:12–18. Many, many years later, you will discover Daniel and the three Hebrew boys: Shadrach, Meshach, and Abed-nego; once again the Jewish people are being forced to disrespect and to disobey God Almighty. The servant Of God, King Nebuchadnezzar, began to become full of himself and spake and said, "Is not this great Babylon, that I have built for the house of the kingdom by the might of my power, and for the honor of my majesty?"

While the words were in the king's mouth, the Voice of the Lord from heaven spake, saying, "O King Nebuchadnezzar, to thee it is spoken; the kingdom is departed from you." Daniel 6:12 also shows how Daniel had to defy the order and the royal decree of the king of the Medes and Persians; that no one should pray a prayer or ask a petition to any god nor of any man for thirty days except to Darius the king or he will be put into the den of lions. This was not going to happen, for Daniel loves to pray and commune to the Holy One of Israel; it was his devout and reasonable worship to his God. So Daniel went home in contempt and, in righteous indignation, opened up his windows toward Jerusalem, and he kneeled down as it was his custom three times a day with prayer and supplication and gave thanks unto the Lord his God.

Daniel 4:32b part is recorded as the Lord speaks to Daniel about King Nebuchadnezzar's self-aggrandizement of himself that "the most high rules in the kingdom of men, and gives to whomever he chooses." In essence, God has total and absolute authority to delegate power, control, and dominion to any man He will, in that case any woman. God, the Father of Abraham, Isaac, and Jacob and the Father of our Lord and Savior Jesus the Christ, have chosen every natural-born human being to their destiny and their lot in life—the good and the bad, the clean vessel, as well the unclean—all have been designed and created by the Potter to do His will. I can't explain it any better other than God is awesome. He is a wonder to perform. Psalm 75:6–7 explains that exaltation or promotion comes neither from the east nor from the west nor from the south. but God is the judge. He puts down one and exalts another. For in the hand of the Lord, there is a cup the Lord kills and makes alive. He brings down to the grave and brings up, the Lord makes poor and He makes rich. He brings low and lifts up. He raises the poor from the dust and lifts the beggar from the ashes; the Lord will set his people among princes and make them inherit the throne of glory.

God orders us to serve as slaves of love. Love is a commitment and a responsibility. In Ephesians 5:21–25, Paul speaks to the church of the Ephesians about love, submission, and humility one to another in the fear of the Lord God. However, this love is the key to all our woes. Love shows our devotion and our responsibility to our fellow man. I am my brother's keeper, and we are responsible, we are liable, we are accountable, we are to be dependable, we are to blame. It is our job, our task, the duty of the loving believer; it is our conscientiousness. Commitment is love as a vow, its love in a pledge, its love in a promise. Commitment is love in loyalty and in faithfulness. Love is dedication, love binding things together in unity as one. We are called to serve God in love and to serve our fellow citizens in love. God has ordained it so; love is the pinnacle and is paramount to the essence of human existence.

Submission and humility are two qualities we talked about in previous chapters and how God uses them to exalt people who stay in a position of submission and humility in love. We submit and humble to one another in the fear of the Lord. To fear is a dual reality and twofold; its duality is the fear of reverence and respect of the spiritual man, and as far as the physical man, we are going to fear God with human emotional frightened ones who's feared and dread the alarm of the terror and horror of eternal damnation death forever in torment; this is our trepidation. However, God has not given us the spirit of fear, meaning God doesn't want us to fear anything nor anyone—no one but God Himself, the Almighty One, which is the beginning of wisdom. Fear God reverently and out of apprehension. Verse 22 of said chapter insists that wives also submit themselves unto their own husband, as unto the Lord. For the husband is head of the wife, even as Christ is the head of the church, and He is the savior of the body. The church is subject unto Christ, so let the wives be subject to their own husbands in everything. It goes on to tell husbands to love their wives even as Christ also loved the church and gave himself for it. Commitment and responsibility, obligation and dependability are our call to God, husbands, wives, and one another. It is our makeup, our DNA. First Timothy 6:1–2 tells us to "All who are under the yoke of slavery should consider their masters worthy of full respect, so that GOD's name and our teaching may not be slandered."

Ordered to serve, we are slaves; at least we should want to be, for a slave gives his will and way over by submitting and depending on his master. Our master, by call and choice, is the God of love, our heavenly Father. As we serve man and his kind, a slave has one purpose, one assignment, one mission, and one task, and that is to please the master by letting our light shine so that men might see our good works and glorify God the Father, who is in heaven. We want to pleasure the Lord our God by keeping and holding up His standards. Under the yoke of restraint, the yoke of temperance, the yoke of meekness, the yoke of our bonds, our demarcation! This yoke is the same yoke God gave to Jeremiah in his day and is the same yoke Jesus gave his disciple and the same yoke we have today. The same as it was in yesteryears, a burden and a task to serve through obedience; obedience is honor to an earthly master so that the true master, the God of the universe, might be honored, and His word, His teaching, His precepts might be adhered for God's will and His way may not be spoken evil of for God's word and promise cannot fail, and He cannot lie nor can He be unfaithful. So we as servants may perform as we have been designed to be and to do. Those men might see the servant honor their master, their Lord, their God, and know that our God, the one and only true and living God, has ordained all things for His good! He is an awesome God, a good God, a wonderful God!

"And they that have believing masters, let them not despise them, because they are brethren; but rather do them service; because they are faithful and beloved; partakers of the benefit. These things teach and exhort. If any man teach otherwise and consent not to wholesome words, even the word of our Lord Jesus Christ, and to the doctrine which is according to godliness." The slaves that have masters that have faith in Jesus should not take advantage of them or misuse, mistreat, and manipulate their kindness, for they are in Christ together as brothers with different tasks but the same God.

Colossians 4:1 says, "Masters give your servants what is just and fair, equal knowing you also have a master in heaven." There should be a working relationship between slave and master to benefit them both, and as Christians, we are to believe as one together in Christ.

Colossians 3:18–25 says, "Wives submit, husbands love, children obey and servants obey a reward to all who serve well from the Lord Jesus Christ." These scripture gives us the order, the structure, and the chain of command for the whole family. There are rules and regulations for a slave and a servant and a son. God has made it that way. What is so wild and amazing about being ordered to serve is that our women and our wives in today's time and engaged couples are abolishing the word *submit* and *obey* from their marriage vows; we want to hate certain words or phrases.

First Peter 5:5–7 conveys that all of His creation—man, woman, boy, and girl—all must submit to God, then you would be able to resist the devil (i.e. resist your eyes, resist yourselves, resist your flesh and your lust). Young folk, submit to your elders, in other words, to your parents and their peers, to your grandparents and their peers, as well as the leaders of the church in the kingdom of God. All of us must be submissive to one another and be clothed in humility for God resists the proud but gives grace to the humble; humble yourselves under the mighty hand of God and He will exalt you. Cast all your cares upon the Lord our God, for He will care for you! This is extreme love and obedience.

First Peter 2:13–17 directs submission to governmental authority.
First Peter 2:18–25 directs submission to our masters.
First Peter 3:1–6 directs submission to husbands.

These three institutions: government-kingdom, master as the employer, as well the teacher, instructor, and last but not least, the husband—all are ordinance of God; all that God has ordained and prescribed for His creation and His masterpiece, the human race.

These scriptures from 1 Peter help establish this chapter, "Order to Serve," and this book, *God Ordained Slavery*!

> Submit yourselves to every ordinance of man for the Lord's sake; whether it be to the king as supreme; or unto governors, as unto them that are sent by him for the punishment of evildoers, and for the praise of them that do well. For so is the will of God, that with well doing ye may put to silence the ignorance of foolish men. As free; and not using your liberty for a cloak of maliciousness, but the servants of God. (1 Peter 2:13–16)

God, the Father of Abraham, Isaac, and Jacob and the Father of our Lord and Savior Jesus the Christ, has ordained government-kingdom, ordinance, and institution for our benefit and for our consequences, good or bad. We are to submit ourselves for the sake of the Lord to every human institution, whether to a king, a prince, governor, or any official officer. Laws are designed to be adhered to and obeyed for governing authority are sent to us by the king or the government-kingdom to enforce the law and punish wrong and evildoers, as well the government-kingdom is also there to honor and praise those who are righteous and uphold the law, good standards, and deeds. If you want the rewards of the authorized institution, you have to submit to that institutional authority that gives ramification, consequences of punishment, as well as the ordinance of man. It is God's will that our good living and our righteous communication be recognized and emulated and that it may silence the ignorance and foolish accusation of men. The Bible tells us that we are not slaves to the world; it states that we are free, so live as free men free from sin and shame, but don't let our freedom be an excuse to do wrong and evil. However, we are free to willfully surrender ourselves to becoming a slave to God in love. Show respect and honor to all people; love the brotherhood. All Christians fear God and honor the king.

Submission to Masters
1 Peter 2:18–25

As for all of us who are working for others, be it the president of a country or a king over a kingdom, we all serve one another and must accept the authority of your master with all respect to do whatever they will us to do, not only to those who are good, gentle, and kind, but reverence to those who are harsh, mean, and unreasonable, for God is pleased and you will find favor.

If a man or woman can bear up under the pain of unjust suffering because he or she is conscious of God's grace and our will to live before the world, we are to endure hardship as good soldiers, for what credit is there if when you sin and do wrong and you are harshly treated, you endure it with patience? There is no benefit, but if you do what is right and suffer for it and you patiently endure it, this finds favor, and God is pleased, and you get a "Well done, good and faithful servant, you have been faithful over a few things. Come on up, and I'll make you ruler over many."

For we have been called for this purpose and ordered to serve. For if you can follow orders well, then you will be able to give them. Since Christ also suffered for us, leaving us an example for us to follow in his steps. Jesus never sinned and never deceived anyone. He did not retaliate when He was insulted; when He suffered, He did not ever threaten to get even. He left His case and His circumstances in the hands of God the Father who judges righteously and fairly, and Jesus personally bore and carried away all of our sins in his own body on the cross so that we can be dead to sin and alive forever in Christ Jesus. For by his wounds and stripes we are healed. We were continually wandering and straying away from the love of God like lost sheep. But now, alleluia! We have returned to our shepherd, our overseer, and the guardian of our souls.

Submission to Husbands
1 Peter 3:1–6

"Likewise ye wives, be in subjection to your own husbands; that, if any obey not the word, they also may without the word be won by the conversation of the wives."

The word *likewise* deals with the previous text as well as in order to serve willfully, submission to the Lord our God. Glory to His name for the victory!

Wives, be in subjection is a command of the Lord from Genesis 3:16, "Unto the woman God said I will multiply thy sorrow and thy conception; in sorrow thou shall bring children; and thy desire shall be to thy husband, and he shall rule over you." The woman in her beguiled state of mind is always vulnerable and will constantly want to be in control of man. Therefore, God orders the woman to serve her husband. This is why earrings and piercing are so common for women around the world, a sign of submission that she may be disciplined under a type of suffering, but the woman is known to be the weakest or, as they say, the weaker vessel. Women need to know their purpose, their ability, and their disability.

> Likewise, ye younger, be subject unto the elder. Yea, all of you gird yourselves with humility, to serve one another: for God resisteth the proud, but giveth grace to the humble. Humble yourselves therefore under the mighty hand of God, that he may exalt you in due time. (1 Peter 5:5–6)

Father God, in the mighty name of Jesus Christ our Lord, we truly thank You for Your wonderful word and wisdom for humble service. Amen.

CHAPTER 5

The Mark
Revelation 22:3–4, 19:20, 20:4

There are marks that every human being will receive in their lifetime whether they want them or not. These marks can come from birth, surgery, vaccination, maybe even gunshot wounds, stabbing, burns, dog bites, or any other kind of accident that may happen to us. Some are even intentionally self-inflicted: marks like hickeys, sexually transmitted diseases (herpes), drug tracks and dimples, tattoos, body piercing, and branding. You know, marks have their own unique story all of their own, stories that tell the history behind every scar, every hole, every mark, and every impression on the body. These marks pinpoint to dates, times, seasons, places, people, groups, gangs, clubs, fraternity, sorority, animals, gadgets, and contrivance. I recall a mark that I foolishly inflicted to myself some thirty-three years ago while I was in the US Marine corps. I was a very arrogant and ignorant young man, and I made a bet that I could hold a one-dollar bill against my wrist and put a lit cigarette against the dollar, and it would burn the dollar before it burned my wrist. You know I received second-degree burns; now I look at my wrist, and I remember the folly of my ways. These are insignia, omens, and stigmas we receive and give to ourselves without knowing the ramifications and the consequences of willingly receiving marks like tattoos, brandings, and any kind of piercings, because these are marks of servitude, submission, obedience, and most of all, humiliation. Yes, we are even enslaving ourselves to a life of service to something or someone; we don't realize what is happening until we are in too deep. However, we need to be wise and more understanding of how this world works through Satan and his tempters as well how they use the lust of the eyes, the pride of life, and the lust of the flesh for our demise. These are powers we fall prey to, and we even truly accept the ways of life and all that goes with it in this mundane world. We will even kill, steal, fight, haze, and even brand ourselves with a hot iron to receive approval of the myriad of worldly organizations, fraternities, gangs, and groups that humans establish through religion, rituals, and traditions. In the Old Testament scripture, Deuteronomy 15:16–17 and Exodus 21:5–7, it expresses ways that a Hebrew person that is poor and in debt can Indenture/enslave themselves temporarily to get out of debt and poverty within the seventh year of jubilee, but some would choose to stay and become a permanent slave with his masters because they love them and had created a family that they didn't want to leave within the six years of the jubilee. The man was unable to take his family if he went into slavery single but could leave without them, but if he wants his family, he would go unto his master, then unto the judge and to the temple to receive the mark, the sign, and/or the omen of his permanent status as a slave: he got his ears pierced. The Old Testament used the words *bore* and *awl*, the tools used to mark all slaves. The mark was for life and forever, so don't give yourselves over to anyone except your true and real eternal master and judge, our God and Father. O how beautiful it is to know that Jesus the Christ our Lord was such a great example, for he was even marked both spiritually as the Lamb of God and physically as the Son of Man, the suffering servant. Jesus, as the Lamb of God, was marked as having no marks on body, spirit, or soul, no sin, no iniquities, and no trespasses—sin free. Jesus was spotless; He was a lamb without a spot or blemish, but the irony of it all is He was to become a lamb bruised and spotted, bruised for our iniquities and spotted with the blood for our atonement. Now Jesus, as the Son of Man, the suffering servant, received the ultimate marks, scars, and holes in his form; His head down to His feet on that auspicious historical Good Friday on that old rugged cross of Calvary, Golgotha Hill. It was the stigma of humility, obedience in humble submission, and servitude.

This is the essential path for all of humanity and especially to every born-again baptized believer in Jesus the Christ, for the church is to bear the stigma of the cross, which is also a burden we must endure. So let's travel the retrospective pages of the spiritual logos and you will discover that it was customary for landlords, landowners, and the masters to mark or brand their personal property, whether it was a horse, an ox, a cow, a sheep, or even human chattel; the owners marked their property and permanent slaves were especially marked and became totally dependent on their master. Psalms 79:13, 95:7, and 100:3 all state, "Know that the Lord, He is God; it is He who made us, and not we ourselves; we are his people and the sheep of his pasture." We are God's property, for He is the Lord of life—all life, all that lives. If you would look at these three scriptures in Psalms, they imply that the people are God's sheep, God's personal property, and the Lord is the Good Shepherd, the Great Shepherd, our Redeemer. Unto him we live, move, and have our being, we must totally trust and depend on Jesus our God! David said it best as a psalmist in Psalm 23: "The Lord is my shepherd, I shall not want. He makes me lie down in green pasture, He leadeth me beside the still waters, and He restores my soul." We as believers must come to the realization and recognize God's Lordship and truly depend on Him totally! Absolutely! God is the real Lord of the ring and the Master of the universe, and we should all make him Lord and Master over our lives. Just as a slave, we must want and choose to submit. Yes, the slave chooses to serve; even if he was taken into slavery, he still has to make the choice to serve or not to serve and/or become a disobedient servant and a rebellious rebel worthy of death by fire. Therefore, when we decide to take his mark that God has for us which will be written in our forehead an omen, aura of the Holy Spirit, we would have willingly agreed to worship and serve God forever (Revelations 22:3–4). However, on the contrary, if we do not submit ourselves and continue to resist God as Lord and Master of our souls, we become reprobates automatically left to our own devices and the peril of our independent life with all its folly. By coming to this, we only enslave ourselves to a world of lust, pride, and flesh. The church is the property of God, and even the world is continually being caught up in the world of vanity of the vanities, whose master is the devil, Satan. He did not make us do anything, just tricked us and deceived our own lustful desires we are tempted by. We must realize our weakness and seek help and power from the Lord, our God, our Father, and correct ourselves through our desires, and if they do not line up with God's word, we will have to besiege the throne of God to help us overcome our wicked ways. Still, some of us have the audacity to follow our own lustful desires and continue to mark our borrowed bodies that God our Maker has given us stewardship over. In the book of Leviticus 19:27–28 KJV, you will discover other traps and tricks Satan uses to deceive us into marking our bodies, our house, our temples of the living God. The scripture quotes, "Ye shall not round or cut the corners of your head; the hair on the side of the head or mar the corners of thy beard which is to trim the beard, ye shall not make any cutting in your flesh for the dead nor print any mark upon you: I am the Lord God."

In essence, God is simply saying don't let your mourning, emotion, and grief cause you to become entangled in perpetual rituals of deception that Satan has designed for us to be overly concerned about the dead. There are individuals, young and old, to this day who are still subscribing to and investing in memorial tattoos for their deceased ones as monuments of worship without knowledge all over their God-given, God-ordained bodies. Romans 12:1–2 NLT states, "And so, dear brothers and sisters, I plead with you to give your bodies to God. Let them be a living and holy sacrifice- the kind He will accept. When you think of what he has done for you, is it too much to ask? Do not copy the behavior and customs of this world, but let God transform you into a new person by changing the way you think. Then you will know what God wants you to do and you will know how good and pleasing and perfect His will really is."

It is our reasonable service, our logical worship, and our rational endeavor to please God the Father. Dead things are for the dead; Satan marks his servant for death and God marks His servants for life! Satan loves misery and is the author of the cliché, "Misery loves company," and so does the joy and peace of God the Father. Satan desires to kill, steal, destroy to get to God's children that we might accompany him to that miserable lake of fire. Nevertheless, our God shall supply all of our needs according to his riches in glory through Christ Jesus. For He is Lord of lords, King of kings, and the God of gods. As if you did not know; now you know that the word *lord* means "owner." According to the Psalms 99 and 100, both verses 2–3, "The Lord expresses himself as the King of the nations and how they tremble and that my throne sits between two cherubim and that the whole earth quake. I also sit in majesty in Zion supreme above all the nations, so let the world praise my great, wonderful, and awesome name for my name is holy. Make a joyful noise and a loud shout unto Me your Lord. O earth, worship Me as Lord with all gladness. Acknowledge the Lord your God! I made you and not you yourselves, you are Mine, My people, the sheep of My pasture." Glory to God for He is sovereign the only wise God, our Savior, the Master of the universe. We are given stewardship over God's property; we do not have ownership over God's handiwork. We and all we have is given to us to glorify, magnify, and to testify of God's mercy, His grace, and His will. We belong to God and God opposes his children marking on his property. God would have you to know that the earth is the Lord's and the fullness thereof the world and they that dwell therein. We are not our own; we are bought with the precious blood of the Lamb, Jesus our Lord. We are marking ourselves with all sorts of graven images, literally cutting, piercing, and poking holes all over our God's perfectly designed creation. Scratching, sketching, etching, stamping, and branding signatures and images completely over our temples, our earthen tabernacle that God the Father ordained. These badges and marks signify servitude to somebody, something, some god, some lord, or some master. We are traveling so far from the will of God and from His intent that we have not recognized the danger all around us and the things we are serving and why. Beginning to act and behave so unruly, so ungodly, caught up, tied up, wrapped up, and tangled up, believing we have control over these things, but all along, it has us in its grips and has become overwhelmed and helpless and ignorant of the tempter. Hosea of the

Old Testament will agree that the people are destroyed for the lack of knowledge. Because we have rejected the knowledge of God. God said, "You reject me. I will reject thee." Why will God reject us? God only rejects us when we are unreceptive, rebellious, and repent not to His will and ways the word and its commandments.

Man has often viewed God's commandment as a stumbling block and foolishness. Man and his kind have always wanted to be sophisticated and intellectuals, having knowledge and wisdom without acknowledging God's omnipotent power and Godhead. Man and his kind are consciously pursuing an agenda to become sophisticated. What does that mean to be sophisticated? The word *sophisticated/ion* is a fascinating word; its concept and etymology is from the Greek root word *sophist*, pronounced safest. The definition defines one as an expert, a wise person, clever, cultured, cultivated, urbane, cosmopolitan, suave, intricate, complex, advanced, and worldly. Further language investigation shows the word *sophisticated/ion* has a flowing reality; it is one of the most divisive and evil words in the English dictionary. Entail deceiver: a wolf in sheep's clothing, something or someone not in its original or natural state, it's not pure, not authentic. Actually, it's deprived of any native simplicity; it's something we made with no radical components. Can you see the sad condition we are engaged in? The human race is possessed with secular ambitions to appear wise and intelligent when we are not. We desire to be scholars, philosophers, lawyers, and doctors without the anointing, calling, or vocation from God's ordination. Just give us a degree for anything honorary; we just want to be recognized. However, it is all without God and His gift of grace, which is unmerited, neither earned nor rewarded. It is the gift of God to be received by Jesus our Savior. Therefore, all this stuff—prestige and reputation—is for naught; it is just spiritual adultery, for without the Holy Spirit and his revelation knowledge and his wisdom, we are just pompous and arrogant pigs like unto their self-elevated master and father of the counterfeit and dubbed the devil himself.

Nimrod is the prototype of the same defect; he is known as a mighty hunter before the Lord, and the beginning of his kingdom was Babel, Erech, Accad, and Calneh in the land of Shinar. From that land, he went to Assyria and built Nineveh, Rehoboth Ir, Calah, and Resen between Nineveh and Calah, which is the principal city (Genesis 10:8–12). Chapter 11:1–4 shows us how they build a reputation or a name for themselves whose top is in the heavens without God in their business. We must study the scripture to see how Eve was tempted, hoodwinked, and subdued by her passions, lusts, and desires to be wise from the tree of knowledge of good and evil in the midst of the garden that would open up her eyes like unto a god! Now thousands of years later, we are still lusting for that same old forbidden, unripe, impure fruit of knowledge without God Almighty's approval. I guess it's true that there is nothing new under the sun; nevertheless, we need God the Father for He has provided provisions for us who want wisdom and knowledge to just ask Him for it. For God gives to all liberally, unrestrained, and unbridled to benefit our lives. Nevertheless, we must first ask in faith, not doubting, because a doubter never receives anything from the Lord. For it is impossible to please God without faith, for He who comes to God must first believe that God is and that He is the rewarder of them that persevere in seeking Him as the Master of the universe. As generation to generation goes on, mankind becomes wiser but weaker—wiser in the world system but weaker in the things of God: weak in love, weak in faith, weak in patience, weak in mercies, just weak. Always consider being so different from one another; diversity is good, but it is also innately unique from our Creator and God. So we don't have to try so hard to appear so different, putting ourselves in the class and mold of clones and clowns with other self-made, self-proclaimed misfits making themselves a dime a dozen, taking away all the intrinsic value God has released in us.

The rebels have marked themselves with the omen of the lost bunch as children graffiti temples tagged not by God. All done by our own choosing and might; truly, our own ignorance because we have chosen to be ignorant, and history has once again proven that it repeats itself, and we have failed to review it carefully.

CHAPTER 6

Two Masters
Matthew 6:24

No man can serve two masters: for either he will hate the one, and love the other; or else he will hold to the one, and despise the other. Ye cannot serve God and mammon.

This is a physics lesson for the spiritual and the physical man that Jesus, the anointed king of glory, gave to Saint Matthew and Sir Isaac Newton to explain the three laws of motion. The force action of motion states that for every action, there is a reaction between two bodies equally opposite and collinear in the same path, as well as how two objects cannot occupy the same space at the same time. These are the fundamentals of physics in our world for the God of heaven and the universe wants us to know how science-knowledge and spirit-metaphysics work together. There are three laws in physics:

1. Velocity: constant moving body—the body in motion stays in motion, the body at rest stays at rest.
2. Acceleration force: $f = ma$—energy, thrust, power, and drive.
3. Action and reaction: for every action, there is a positive or negative reaction.

And our God and Father operates in all three ways. You can see God the Father in the velocity of the constant moving motion body of faith, the ever cresting in faith. Then there is Jesus Christ, the Son of God, the accelerating force of hope, the momentum changer, and there is the Holy Ghost, the action of God and the reaction of love. The physics and the metaphysics both illuminate Matthew 6:24 crystal clear.

No man, no woman, no boy, no girl, no human, nobody, and no one, absolutely none of humanity, unequivocally, no man will be able to serve two masters. It is a futile endeavor; however, man has the propensity to try anything, but to serve both is not possible. It is just not a part of our makeup or our DNA. Even if our children fail to obey what both father and mother order them to perform at the same time, there will be much confusion and discord in the family. First, the father and mother must operate as parents in the spirit of unity as one in order to receive the maximum and optimal effect intended. Therefore, it is with a servant-steward and his master that a servant cannot take two commands in succession or simultaneously from two different individuals and be worth anything of value. The servant today or even those from the past might be able to multitask, but soon down the line, one of the two will be neglected and mistreated. For there is a love-hate relationship in serving and obeying two principals. We cannot serve God and mammon, or our provider and possessions, or the Lord and wealth, nor the king and greed. There will be a tug-of-war going on in the human race, a great dilemma for us because we think both are necessities. The only thing in this world that gives the God of the universe any slight competition for dependency with humanity is mammon, money, wealth, riches, and possessions. These are our nemeses; we continue to struggle with our concerns and care for our individual independence. While God said, "I got this!"

Jesus teaches us how to live in a world of uncertain financial portfolios without the stress and fear of nonbelievers. We, as the children of God, are not to become distracted from the substantial issues of life. The word of God tells us not to take thought for our lives, what we shall eat, or what we shall drink; neither for our bodies, what shall we put on, for the God over the entire universe is the Creator and our Father, and he cares for us. Glory to his name! Here is the million-dollar question: is not your life more than meat (food) and the body more than raiment (clothes)? You should see how the birds of the air neither sow seeds nor reap and gather into barns, yet our heavenly Father feeds them. Are we not much more than the fowls? Don't allow mammon to master you by choosing to serve it; instead of God, our choice of masters is not solely an issue of prudence nor a choice of priorities nor is it a mere question of responsibility or our moral choice. Rather, it is a clear issue of impossibility that we have no choice. We must choose to serve God and to have mammon subjected to us. We are to love the Lord God the Father of our Lord and Savior Jesus Christ who has given to us eternal life.

Be loyal to God as single-minded devoted servants, forsaking all personal ambitions that compromise our commitment and service to God. Acknowledge worry and anxiety as sin; discipline yourselves by turning from any anxiety, and choose to serve and trust the living Lord.

First Timothy chapter 6 expounds on how to honor one master:

> Let as many bondservants as are under the yoke count their own master worthy of all honor, so that the name of the God and His doctrine may not be blasphemed. And those who have believing masters, let them not despise them because they are brethren, but rather serve them because those who are benefited are believers and beloved. Teach and exhort these things. (Verses 1–2)

Error Teaching and True Riches

> If anyone teaches otherwise and does not consent to wholesome words, even the words of our Lord Jesus Christ, and to the doctrine which accords with godliness, he is proud, knowing nothing, but is obsessed with disputes and arguments over words, from which come envy, strife, reviling,

evil suspicions, useless wrangling of men of corrupt minds and destitute of the truth, who suppose that godliness is a means of gain. From such withdraw yourself. Now, godliness with contentment is great gain. For we brought nothing into this world, and it is certain we can carry nothing out. And having food and clothing, with these we shall be content. But those who desire to be rich fall into temptation and a snare, and into many foolish and harmful lusts, which drown men in destruction and perdition. For the love of money is the root to all kind of evil; for which some have strayed from the faith in their greediness, and pierced themselves through with many sorrows. But you O man of God, flee these things and pursue righteousness, godliness, faith, love, patience, gentleness." (Verses 3–11)

This pericope, the text framework, and its context elaborate on the Christians who are slaves-employees of the first or the twenty-first century should give their unsaved masters-employers full respect so that the name of God and His teaching and our faith will not be slandered and that Christians masters-employers do not disrespect their slaves-employees. "Believer blessing believers"—these principles are to be edified, preached, and taught to all of God's people. Equality in the body of Christ does not cancel differences of function and place in the church or in society. Paul reverts to the necessity of sound doctrine; all teaching is to be judged by its agreement with the unadulterated word of our Lord Jesus Christ. Some teachers', some preachers', some pastors', bishops', some elders' egos are inflated by their own importance, having substituted contentious doctrine and splitting hairs from the wholesome teaching of Christ with a pure conscience. Some make arguments that are useless and totally unprofitable, and there are those who always cause trouble by inciting controversy because their minds are corrupt and distorted. To them, religion and godliness is just a way to get rich for the sake of gain; we are to have no religious fellowship with them that would close many convocations. Godliness is synonymous with true religion, with righteousness, with justice, and with holiness. True religion: Godliness with contentment is great wealth, and it should be enough to satisfy us. However, these powerful scriptures are being overlooked for some strange reason. In Christendom, contentment is not being preached nor taught as its counterpart: prosperity as in wealth and not in rich in well doing, rich in love, rich in faith, and rich in mercy. Not proud and foolishly in love with riches to covet after our demise, but we are to trust in the living God, who gives to us richly all things to enjoy; God gives to us! That we do good, that we are rich in good works, ready to distribute, willing to communicate. Riches are a responsibility, and wealthy people should be good stewards in sharing with others. Distributing it is an eternal investment yielding great dividends. With these verses, we can avoid a lot of misunderstanding and hardships about the acquisition of wealth and material goods.

Paul, the apostle of Jesus Christ, tells us not to trust in uncertain riches. We are not to hope, trust, nor expect riches to bring us security or deliverance. This doesn't sound like the prosperity message that is going around in the ecumenical community today, and Paul would not agree with this rudiment teaching. Why do I state that? Because riches are so transient, the values consistently change, and earthly riches are only as good as the present value. The dollar today is no longer backed up by gold and is inflated, so what's valuable today might not be valuable tomorrow; thus the wisdom of our trusting, putting our hope in God alone to make provision for us. It further warns us that we must never let the presence of wealth make us think that we are better or above anyone. Or that we can be irresponsible by indulging in things like buying three-hundred-thousand-dollar automobiles or fifty-thousand-dollar watches, rings, or two-thousand-dollar suits and shoes while the members are without and in need.

What really is the problem? Ten or twenty parishioners that travel on the city bus could be a blessing with their own car or, in that case, have employment for a year with such a budget, but we would rather misappropriate funds for our own benefit. Wealth is a great responsibility, and we must always remember that to whom much is given to those much is required. We must lay up for ourselves a good foundation against the time to come, that we may lay hold to eternal life. It is said a good foundation is not a well-funded account; after all, we did not bring anything with us when we came into the world, and it is certain we will carry nothing out with us. Therefore, if we have enough food and clothing, you need to be content because the material needs are neither the reason nor the measure of our joy or contentment. The love of money is a restless desire for those who would be rich and will subject themselves into great spiritual danger. Loving money (mammon) opens one's lives to the ultimate deception. The apostle Paul clearly points out how we should relate to money, wealth, and the price of being deceived by the love of it. For there is nothing inherently wrong with wealth or money. It is to be mastered working as a slave to serve us and others, but it can become problematic when we think money answers all things, spiritually and physically, and becomes the source of all things then we are in clear and present danger. We are to have one Master, one Lord, one Savior, one God, and one King, and they are all in one immortal, blessed, and potentate person, Jesus the Christ! There are three examples that we need to glean, explore, and establish. One story deals with the rich young ruler in the book of Matthews 19:16–26. Read it, and you will discover the rich young ruler is trying to worship and serve both God and mammon, believing that eternal life can be earned either from his good upbringing or his deep pockets; however, neither will do. Therefore, Jesus directs his attention to God, the only one that is good! And no one can keep a perfect law perfectly except Jesus, for it is impossible for a mortal man to keep a holy law, but with God, all things are possible. This is why salvation is by grace and not by works. Jesus tries again to lead the young man to the right path with a stern challenge designed to show the young man that he has not observed the spirit of the commandment in spite of his claims. In fact, his selfish attitude in making mammon (possessions) an idol violates the first commandment in Exodus 20:3, "You shall have no other gods before Me,' said God."

"What good thing must I do to be saved?" the young man asked.

Jesus replied, "There is one thing you can do: sell all your possessions and give the money to the poor, and you will have riches in heaven and follow Me."

This was a devastating blow to the rich young ruler because he wanted to go to heaven with his possessions, and Jesus told him to sell it all, and he could not and went away from Jesus sorrowful. The rich young ruler could not depart from the one thing he loved more than God, and that was his possession, his stuff, his prestige, and his comfort. Let God do the impossible, for He has the power and the ability to make all things well. God and his son Jesus cannot come second to none, to anything or anyone. God wants all or nothing at all! Therefore, we need to love one and hate one and be loyal to the one you love in this two-master-occupied society.

The next example comes from the book of Luke 19:1–10, and its narrative is on Zacchaeus, the small but rich notorious tax collector, greedy of fealty to lucre, employed by the Roman government as a chief publican. Now publicans were both publicly and religiously outcast because they were viewed as cooperating with the Roman occupational government. Their bad tax-collecting practices and their exorbitant amount of interest and usury made them hated; nevertheless, Zacchaeus wanted to see Jesus; the miracle worker; the man everyone was talking about. You know the story of the man short in stature and how he climbed the sycamore tree to get a glimpse of Jesus. Not knowing that Jesus as well came to see him. Jesus called Zacchaeus to come down out of the tree because today, salvation is present in Jesus. He has come to save that which was lost, and Zacchaeus was lost, just like others who had demons and those healed of all manner of diseases. The power of the kingdom was there to spend a night at Zacchaeus's house, and Zacchaeus came down in a hurry to welcome Jesus into his home. With great joy, he humbled himself and told Jesus that he would give half of his possessions to the poor, and if he had cheated anyone, he would pay it all back four times as much. This evidence of change and repentance of heart goes up and beyond the law of restitution required (Leviticus 6:1–5). Jesus said to Zacchaeus, "Salvation has come to this house today!"

Zacchaeus desired to give away his stuff to show that he loved Jesus with his whole heart much more than mammon. Zacchaeus hated and despised the wrong he had done for mammon, and he repented and served Jesus as Lord and savior of his soul.

The last narrative is also in the book of Luke 12:13–21, and it's about the rich fool. What can we say about a rich fool, but to watch out and guard your heart from his kind of greed and covetousness. This fool just loved to death his goods, his stuff, his lifestyle. He was a true servant of mammon and was loyal to his master for where your treasure is, there will your heart and love be also. Mammon is a temporal god; it will eventually falter and end, but to trust in one's richness leads to eternal damnation. This man was an eternal fool, for he said, in your heart, there is no God and he loves death. Life is not made up of the thing you own or your possessions; no matter how rich you may be, you will end up in hell. This man was so rich that he thought he was God himself as if he did not need God. He lived and spoke as if he produced the water for the ground to grapple with the soil and made the sun to shine, incubating the soil to bring forth life. This fool lived in a "me, myself, and I" state of mind so much that he edged God out of his program.

Ego. We are either going to love one God/Jesus is eternal or hate mammon and choose God's son and live forever. Our riches, treasure, and wealth are in heaven where our hearts are with our God. We are commanded to hate the devil and the world's system in which Satan is the prince of the air. Ecclesiastes 3:8 informs us that there is a time to love and a time to hate, and it means real hate denotes to despise, to detest, to abhor, and to loathe. Proverbs 8:13 tells us what to hate: "Honor and fear the Lord our God is to hate evil: pride, arrogant, and the evil way, the forward mouth." So if God hates these things, then we are to hate them as well. Hate the evil way; that's the world and the lust thereof. First John 2:15 states, "Not to love the world which is also known as the evil way and if any man loves the world the love of the Father God is not in him. For all that is in the world the lust of the flesh, the lust of the eyes, and the pride of life is not of God; but is of the world. The evil way and this world shall pass away, and the inordinate desire and craving thereof with it; but he that loves God does the will of God and they shall live forever. Let not sin therefore reign or control in your mortal body, that you should obey it in the lust thereof. Neither yield your members as instruments of unrighteousness unto the sin of mammon; But yield yourselves unto God, as those that are alive from the dead, and your members as instruments of righteousness unto God."

We can't serve two masters for our God is a jealous God, and He wants all or nothing at all; let me rephrase that for there is no nothing at all in God; God wants all and all because He created it all—100 percent the whole of the total! Absolutely everything: total love, total loyalty, total dependency, total worship, and total praise. God has made it very clear, saying, "I am the Lord thy God, your Sovereign King. Thou shall have no other gods before Me in the heavens above or the earth below or in the water, under the earth. Thou shall not bow down thy self to any graven images. I am a jealous God, simply meaning I will not tolerate any rivalry. I will visit with divine intervention those that love me for a thousand generations and to the sin who hate Me and their descendants down to the third and fourth generation." It was possible for four generations to live around the aged head of the family, because of the close ties of a patriarchal family, the influence of the grand and great-grandparents, good or bad, affected all generations under their control. God the Father will bring punishment on those who choose to serve two masters or another god.

"You hate Me when you serve two masters or another god, and I will bring turmoil to your family tree for sixty to eighty years." A generation is twenty years, and twenty years multiplied by three or four is a long time to curse or destroy our offspring by serving two masters or other gods. This is a warning that spiritually impacts our decisions made or our actions taken and how it is transmitted to succeeding generations. While no child is held responsible for the sins of their forefathers, they might inherit a propensity to engage and entangle themselves in a yoke of bondage the power that perpetuates its evil consequences delivered onto our children. Worldly lust and the love of money and possession will demand all of our attention, loyalty, and time that should belong to glorifying, praising, and serving God our Father.

Ecclesiastes 10:19 NIV says, "A feast is made for laughter, and wine makes life merry, but money is the answer for everything." You cannot have a feast (laughter) nor wine (makes merry) without money and/or those possessions and those that have it retain the options to do what they please. Christendom likes to quote and use this verse to get the congregants to buy into the worldly concept of the value of money because it is carnality and comes from King Solomon's allusions of wisdom and his unrighteous writing of his personal journeys. His quests through wisdom, wealth, servants, pleasures, and winebibber experiences have given to us an earthly wisdom, but it is not the teaching of our Lord and Savior Jesus the Christ that promotes Matthew 6:33, "Seek first the Kingdom of God and His righteousness and all these thing will be added unto you." Rather than being preoccupied with material things causing anxiety, stress, and pressure. Jesus speaks clearly against worry and anxiety because of the loving watchful care of God our heavenly Father who is always mindful of our daily needs. Our only goal, desire, and ambition should be to seek God first and his kingdom of righteousness, knowing as we do so. God has promised Himself with the covenant of faithfulness to respond and reward our diligence. God requires that we love less—that is to hate mother, father, sister, and brother and love Him above all others for the love you express for your loved ones should pale in comparison to the love we have for our heavenly Father and shall come in at a very far second. The love for our loved ones should be equivalent to hate. The church body is flirting with this same situation and dilemma. We want to preach the prosperity message without the warning of its dangers and its responsibility. You will prosper when you know the truth about God the Father, the Supplier of all our needs, according to His riches in glory in Christ Jesus! The third epistle of John is always misinterpreted as a prosperity and godliness is great gain scripture without the true intent of the word.

> The elder unto the well beloved Gaius whom I love in truth. Beloved, I wish above all things that thou mayest prosper and be in health, even as thy soul prospereth. For I rejoiced greatly, when the

brethren came and testified of the truth that is in thee, even as thou walkest in the truth. I have no greater joy than to hear that my children walk in truth. Proper in the Truth of God living word your whole Being.

The Double-Minded Man
A Profit from Our Trials
James 1:2–8

"A double minded man is unstable in all his ways" (verse 8). This man or person is someone pulled in two opposite directions. His allegiance is divided, and because of his lack of sincerity, they vacillate between belief and disbelief, between love and hate, between honor and dishonor, and between service and non-service. Such a person is very unstable in all his ways and lacking in the consistency in exercising his faith, betraying his basic character. A double-minded man is a two-master man; he is a two-opinion man, a two-faced man, a wishy-washy man, an up-and-down man, an in-and-out man, a right-and-wrong man, a manic-and-depressed man, a confused man, an uncertain man, An undependable man. Well, you get the picture. The bottom line is this person is just spiritually bipolar, schizophrenic, unfaithful, untrustworthy, and an unreliable human being. So we need to develop a love-hate relationship. We are to love the Lord our God with all your heart, mind, body, and soul and hate sin, mammon, and the Devil Satan who subsidizes sin in the world through covetousness and greed and lust. Love the thing God loves and hate the thing God hates.

Two Worlds: Visible and Invisible
The Bipolar Christian
Colossians 1:16; 2 Corinthians 4:16–18

For by him were all things created; that are in heaven and that are in the earth; visible and invisible, whether they be thrones, or dominions, or

> principalities, or powers, all things were created by him and for him. (Colossians 1:16)

> For which cause we faint not; but though our outward man perish, yet the inward man is renewed day by day. For our light affection, which is but a far more exceeding and eternal weight of glory. While we look not at the things which are seen, but at the things which are not seen; for the things which are seen are temporal but the things which are not seen are eternal. (2 Corinthians 4:16–18)

Here we have two letters written by Paul the apostle; in both letters, the content is similar. They both express the false teachers and detractors in the church. However, the book of Colossians is a unique epistle; it's the only book in the New Testament that fully defines and defends Jesus's universal lordship as the anointed king of glory. This book clearly portrays Jesus as superior and preeminent over all things in creation, visible and invisible, even the negative power in the cosmic. In 2 Corinthians, these three verses allow us to see the invisible things of God, but how can we see the invisible things of God but by faith? The inward man sees more than the outward man that's perishing can. We must clearly see temporary things in the light of eternal things. Do not lose heart because of faith in the future resurrection. Paul's hardship can be termed light affliction, only in comparison with the future eternal weight of God's glory. God is calling four-hundred-plus years of the Israelites enslaved in Egypt a light affliction and almost four hundred years of Africans enslaved in America and Europe a light affliction; yes, even your pain and mine are just light afflictions in comparisons to eternity, joy, and glory with the Lord Jesus. Two worlds, visible and invisible, the outer man and the inner man, the bipolar connection, North Pole versus the South Pole and its pull. The word *bipolar* is defined as having or involving the use of two poles, relating and associated with two polar regions. Listening to be bipolar is to have or to be marked by two mutually repellent forces or diametrically opposed natures or views completely opposed a contradiction. We all live in two worlds, a visible physical world that is engaged when our outward man employs his five perishing senses. Seeing, feeling, smelling, hearing, and tasting—all systems go and work well in the physical temporal world. Then we have the invisible, metaphysical, spiritual world, the inward man. This is the hard one for many of us as human beings. To understand, we would rather dismiss the spiritual world rather as nothing but superstition, a religious practice, the unknown, faithless fear; others however acknowledge the existence of the spiritual world, but believe it has little, if any, influence on them. The truth is the world of the supernatural/spiritual is more real and eternal than the physical temporal world. The spiritual world is the realm from which the physical world came from originally. Our texts tell us by him, Jesus, were all that are on earth, visible and invisible, whether they be thrones-kings or dominions-kingdoms or principalities-ruler or power-authority. All things were created by Jesus and for him. Jesus tells us in the gospel of John 18:36 that his kingdom-government system is not of this world, but if it were, His servants would fight to prevent his arrest by the Jews, but *now*, my kingdom is not of this world. The *now* in this sentence is a timeless word that transcends all time and seasons. For now is now at this very moment is now, now tomorrow will be now, and now in the future will be now. So now refer to the scripture in the book of Revelation 19:15, "And out of his mouth goeth a sharp sword, that with it he should smite the nations; and he shall rule them with a rod of iron and he treads the winepress of the fierceness and wrath of Almighty God."

So then, what world is his kingdom from? He is from the invisible, eternal, spiritual world of God the Father, the world that will be in the now. There are two worlds. Ephesians 6:12 conveys to us that we fight not against flesh and blood people but against the evil ruler and authorities of the unseen world, against those mighty powers of darkness who rule this world, and against wicked spirits in the high-places in the heavenly realms. Listen, it is not a physical fight against another human being, but we do fight the good fight of faith. Our views and beliefs in Christ Jesus against the world's views and beliefs in secularism, humanism, and materialism. Two worlds and its bipolar citizens are Christians. We live in two worlds: body in one world pole system, and the spirit, heart, mind, and soul in another world pole system. The bipolar Christian must stand strong in the Lord Jesus and be victorious. Even when we are weak, we must say that we are strong; the bipolar Christian is to be humble but bold. We are to be servants and kings; we are to be the tail of jokes but the head of states. Bipolar Christians are to abased and yet abound. We are dead to sin but alive in Christ; we are to be last but first, poor but rich. Bipolar Christians are sinners and saints saved by grace. We are corruptible yet clothed in incorruption; we are mortal but will put on immortality! So we grapple as wretched men and women, boys and girls, to be freed and rescued from this body of death, this body of sin, this vessel of hate, this container of diseases, this old dilapidated house, this dirt puppet, this shell of lust, this flesh of lies, and this slave that must be humiliated, subjected, and abased. But thanks be to God, for the antidote is in Jesus the Christ of Nazareth. He is the answer. He's our prescription, the medicine that heals and reconciles the two worlds back together, as it was from the beginning when God walked on earth in the cool of the day with Adam and the two worlds worked together in harmony.

So now we know as Christians, we do all things without murmuring, without complaining, without arguing, and without disputing that we may be blameless. We are to live clean and innocent lives as children of God in this dark world full of crooked and perverse people. So we are to let our little light shine so brightly before men in this old dark world, and God will get the glory. Paul holds up two worlds and two pictures of his dual world, one picture of a boastful spiritual life in Christ upward bound into the heavens, caught up into the third heavens, and heard words never to be articulated. Paul could speak in seventeen different languages more than most people could, and on top of that, signs and wonders followed him, as well as revelation and visions. Yet Paul was able to see both sides of the world; he was a person who would impress anyone's interest in the higher highs and in the deeper depths of spiritual life in God. The other world is the picture of a suffering servant downward and humiliated, a common man full of frailty of the human needs and weakness.

The thorn that is in Paul's flesh demonstrates the glory of God for when we are weak, then are we made strong in the spirit. Do you have a thorn in your flesh? In this physical world, it requires that we have a thorn in our flesh for the thorn naturalizes our fleshly pride. The flesh is the world and the world is the flesh, so God must destroy the fleshly world for it must die, for flesh and the blood cannot inherit the kingdom of God and heaven. The flesh and the world is the body of sin, and Jesus was cursed to take away our sins and the sins of the world. Jesus wore a crown of thorns, for he is the King of the thorn people's kingdom of thorns. For Jesus precedes us in our downward humiliation, He wore the thorns and exchanged it for a crown of pure gold and lived forever in eternal triumph!

My prayer is that we will know the time and season of higher highs and of humble lows for Jesus said, "My grace is sufficient for my power is made perfect in weakness for our light affliction which is but for a moment worketh for us a far more exceeding and eternal weight of glory!" Keep yourselves unspotted from the world, and let the brother of low degree rejoice in that he is exalted and the rich in that he is made low. We are not to love the world nor its very infrastructure and its system for all that's in the world is not of the father but of the devil's world. The pride of life, the lust of the flesh, and the lust of the eyes is Satan's trap are to keep us worldly and carnal in the South Pole downward motion, forever toiling, forever scrapping, and forever grappling in a defeated victimized existence. However, God's great purpose is that we be holy as He is holy and have dominion to colonize the earth with like-minded people in relationship with the Lord God, our Father.

In 1974, the group called the Persuaders had a hit song called "It's a Thin Line between love and hate." Without a doubt, God would say no, there is a gulf fixed between love. God the Father, the lover of our soul, and the devil, the hated one, our enemy. Man just loves to smooth worldly things over to fit our fancy. Love is the mountaintop and Zion Hill, and hate is the depth of the sea. Hades is a very faraway gulf with no line!

Love suffers long and is kind; love does not envy; love does not parade itself, is not puffed up; does not behave rudely, does not seek its own, is not provoked, think no evil; does not rejoice in the iniquity, but rejoices in the truth; love bears all things, love believes all things hopes all things endures all things. Love never fails… But the greatest of these is Love. (1 Corinthians 13:4–8a, 13b)

CHAPTER 7

Choose Ye This Day Whom You Will Serve
Joshua 24:14–16

Now therefore fear the Lord, and serve him in sincerity and in truth; and put away the gods, which your fathers served on the other side of the flood, and in Egypt; and serve ye the Lord. And if it seem evil unto you to serve the Lord, choose you this day whom ye will serve whether the gods which your fathers served that were on the other side of the flood, or the gods of the Amorites, in whose land ye dwell; but as for me and my house we will serve the Lord. And the people answered and said, "God forbid that we should forsake the Lord, to serve other gods."

Human life is full of choices, decisions, assessments, judgments, resolutions, and verdicts. All this has to do with our observation, as we watch to see what is offered and then we inspect by scrutinizing what is heard, and we study by examining what has been spoken or said.

We must choose in this game called life; it is our greatest privilege and opportunity as intelligent God-fearing human beings. God the Father created humanity like himself, in His image and likeness, and has given us a free spirit to act upon our selection and our choice to pick between the two natural forces. Our relationship is predicated on our understanding to prefer God as our maker, the lover of our soul, our heavenly Father, over Satan the devil, the Deceiver, the father of liars, our tempter, and enemy. Nevertheless, choose we must, no limbo status, no gray area, no lukewarm—it's either hot or cold, white or black, light or darkness, or you will forfeit your choice, and if not for Him, your choice will be made for you and you will not like the results or its consequences. In God, there is absolutely no gray area, and if there are, any shades of gray, Satan, the world, or the man put it there to form and add confusion; the devil would rather we stay or stagnate and be idle and our God is not the author of confusion. God made all things good and very good, and God created bad and evil, but He had nothing to do with being lukewarm nor mediocrity. In God's sight, you are either hot or cold, black or white, up or down, right or wrong, love or hate, day or night, faith or doubt. Choose you this day. It is your prerogative, but you must choose either the loving God of the universe or the opposing devil of hell in his eternal residence, the consuming lake of fire.

"Now fear the Lord, and serve him in sincerity and in truth." The word *now* is relative to *chronoes* and *arereos*, times and seasons Now is present at all times; it's in the moment is now. Now is current, now is instant, now is modern; it's contemporary, and it's immediate! Whatever the time or season is it's now; nowadays, fear God now! Now therefore fear the Lord, therefore, for this reason or as a result of all of God's many rich blessings He has bestowed and done through his benevolence for us, for you, and for me, we ought to respect, love, admire, and fear the Lord as God Almighty and Him alone. How can we not? When we fear the Lord with veneration, we will surrender, obey, depend, and serve the Lord our God! In sincerity and truth by being authentic, serious, legitimately genuine, and totally devoted. Absolutely putting away all idols, all gods, all images, not even what God made, the celestial or terrestrial nor man-made, handmade, Egypt-made, nor world-made. How be it gold, silver, bronze, steel, wood, and stones, thou shall have nothing except the Lord God of Abraham, Isaac, and Jacob, and the Father of our Lord and Savior Jesus Christ and Him alone!

Like Elijah in the book of 1 Kings 18:21, he seems to be pushing for a clear-cut decision from the people of Israel, but they answered Elijah not a word. For double mindedness puts a curse on the people of Israel throughout most of their history. Deuteronomy chapter 28 furnishes us with a visual and the opportunity to choose the blessing of obedience or the curses of disobedience. Joshua, Elijah, and Moses's three witnesses knew that part-time service to God is not service at all. Joshua uses the power of example as psychology to the people by saying, "You can do, as you will. Nevertheless, as for my house, and me we will serve the Lord." This evokes from the people a burst of enthusiasm for the worship of the God of Israel. Now Joshua drives and demands their decision deeper; he tells them that no superficial choice will be of any significance. God is a holy and a jealous God; He will not tolerate vacillation nor waffling, for it is a serious offense to make a covenant with God and not to keep it. To break a covenant after entering into it with God will result in destruction on our part. We must think twice and then think it over again before you make a vow with the Lord God, for God will not hold you guiltless. Joshua's caution to Israel had its desired effect, for the people agreed, affirmed, and were willing to serve the Lord as their God only. The word of God designates one picked, one choice, and one selection for all people, especially the people of God; we are to choose to seek first the domain of God and his righteous justice, and all the world is yours for the taking. Out from among the larger group for special service of privileges, it describes Christ Jesus as the chosen one the Messiah, and we believers as the recipients of God's favor.

> I charge thee before God, and the Lord Jesus Christ, and the elect angels, that thou observe these things without preferring one before another, doing nothing by partiality. (1 Timothy 5:21)

> The elect and except those days should be shortened, there should no flesh be saved; but for the elect's sake those days shall be shortened. (Matthews 24:22)

God's elect who shall lay anything to the charge of
God's elect? It is God that is justifieth. (Romans
8:33)

Put on therefore, as the elect of God, holy and
beloved, bowels of mercies, kindness, humbleness
of mind, meekness, longsuffering; forbearing one
another, and forgiving one another, if any man
have a quarrel against any even as Christ forgive
you, so also do ye. And before all these things put
on charity, which is the bond of perfectness. And
let the peace of God rule in your hearts, to which
also ye are called in one body; and be ye thankful.
(Colossians 3:12–15)

How long will you falter?

How long will you halt between two opinions? If the Lord be
God, follow Him, but if Baal is God, then follow him, and the people answered him not a word

Bloodwash or Brainwash: The Contrast

From the very beginning of time and the nativity of the church,
there have always been false teachers and teaching and many distrac-
tions that surround Christendom and even unusual religious activities
and rituals have made the body of believers feel uneasy about some
doctor or scholar having put into the mind the maze of theology.
However, believers and followers of Christ do not become sidetracked
by the insight of religious cults or modern-day philosophies and legalism. Don't be troubled; keep your focus on Christ through prayer,
Bible reading and studying, and good Christian fellowship. The center of our faith, however, should always be Jesus Christ of Nazareth,
our Lord and Savior, the only Person who warrants our allegiances
and trust! Let's see how one can become brainwashed and/or bloodwashed. Leviticus 17:11, 16:11–19 informs us that the life of every
living thing is in the blood, and that is why the Lord has command

that all blood be poured out on the altar to take away the people's sin. Atonement takes the blood of bulls and goats and sprinkles it seven times on the altar to purify the most holy place, the tent, as well as the people of God. Scientists say blood is the body's transportation system that not only carries vital oxygen from the lungs to every cell in the body, it also carries all the food needed to fuel and maintain each cell, and the blood washes away all the waste from the liver, kidneys, and lungs for disposal. It helps spread body heat too. It even plays a crucial role in the body's defense against disease. Hebrews 9:12–14 tells us when Christ went through the tent and entered once and for all into the Most Holy Place, he did not take the blood of goats and bulls to offer a sacrifice; rather, he took his own blood and obtained eternal salvation for us. Jesus is the sacrificial lamb; since this is true, how much more the blood of Christ accomplishes. Through the eternal spirit, He offered himself as a perfect sacrifice to God. His blood will purify our consciences from useless, dead works and rituals, which are religious acts so that we may serve the living God.

"This is the covenant that I will make with them in the days to come," said the Lord. "I will put my laws in their hearts and write them on their minds." This here is a bloodwashed believer! God wants Holy Ghost–filled, Jesus's blood–washed, oracle-speaking, word-professing, decree-claiming, and declaration-prophesied baptized believers in Jesus Christ. Our blood has a voice, and it speaks. According to Genesis 4:10, after Cain murdered Abel, Abel's blood cried out from the grave. Blood speaks loud and clear.

Brainwash human beings. Inside our heads, we carry the most amazing structure in the universe; it is the human brain, and it looks a little like no more than a large soggy gray walnut with all its wrinkled surface. However, within this soft massive sponge are billions of interlinked nerve cells. There are 100 billion cells in the human brain, each connected to as many as 25,000 other cells throughout the body, so there are 25,000 times 100 billion nerve connections in your brain and body or two and a half million billion—awesome. The chemical and electrical impulses whizzing through all these cells create all your thoughts, record every sensation, and control nearly all your actions. The brain demands huge amounts of energy and brain cells;

it also depends on much oxygen in the blood. The brain makes up less than 3 percent of the body's weight, yet it demands more than 25 percent of its blood supply. If the blood supply to your brain were cut off, you would lose consciousness within ten seconds and die within minutes. Your mind is all your thoughts put together as well your emotions, your will, your attitude, your personality, and your imagination. Hebrews 9:14 says the blood supply purifies, purges, cleanses our consciences. Some people love to play games with other people's minds and their psyche by altering a person's consciousness, a process by which one's beliefs and actions are changed extraordinarily. Usually through ideas and suggestions and the use of stress (by keeping them in deprived situations), such as too little sleep and by starvation of food or by exhausting them with constant talking over and over for long periods of time, weeks, or sometimes months. This is known as brainwashing. The term originated in the early 1950s during the Korean War. It means to get rid of or to wash the mind of its beliefs so that others' ideas, thoughts, and suggestions can be substituted. The technique of brainwashing was used by the Chinese Communist Party on American prisoners of war and servicemen and was able to induce a number of prisoners to admit publicly that they had been fighting for an unjust cause and were ready to accept communism.

So from the Korean War experience, we have learned much about the methods of indoctrination. Indoctrination is a word we need to highlight in both areas of these subjects: brainwashing and bloodwashing. The instruction in doctrine or belief to train and accept a system of thought uncritically. There are four conditions that must exist before brainwashing is successful:

1. There must be complete control by those doing the brainwashing over rewards and punishments;
2. Control over all communications such as phone calls, texts, letters, and talking to others.
3. Provides an atmosphere of distrust among one's peers through an informer-mole system; and
4. Separations of the individuals from all normal routines or freedoms.

This is truly the style, work, and action of Satan, the devil, to confuse, divide, and conquer (Compton's Encyclopedia).

There are also biblical terms to describe brainwashing and can be found in the book of Galatians 3:1–5:

> O foolish Galatians, who hath bewitched you, that ye should not obey the truth, before whose eyes Jesus Christ hath been evidently set forth, crucified among you? This only would I learn of you, received by the Spirit by the works of the law, or by the hearing of faith? Are ye so foolish? Having begun in the Spirit, are ye now made perfect by the flesh? Have ye suffered so many things in vain? If it is still in vain. He therefore ministereth to you the Spirit, and worketh miracles among you, doeth He do it by the works of the law, or by the hearing of faith?

1. O foolish Galatians, how simple can you be? You are so easily misguided that you have become the victims of ignorance and irrational decision. Who has brainwashed you not to obey the truth of the gospel? We know it was Satan, the father of the lie. That's just his motive of operation; however, how did you allow yourselves to be bewitched so very soon, having the evidence of the Holy Ghost to help you see Jesus by faith? What spell did the Judaizers cast on you that you would disrespect and disregard the word of God?

2. Paul wants to know one thing about the Galatians: he asked them how they received the Holy Ghost; was it by keeping the law? Of course not; you know it was the Holy Spirit that came upon you. Only and then you believed what you have heard about Christ. I know I taught you the truth about Jesus the Christ! I know you accepted the Lord Jesus as your personal Savior, the fulfillment of the law, full of grace and truth.

3. How can you be so blinded that you lose your mind? You started your Christian journey full of the Holy Spirit; how are you now trying to become perfect and attain your goals through human effort and fleshly works? We are made perfect in the Spirit of God's love and not in anything we do or do not do in the flesh; we are God's children by faith in His Son, Jesus the Christ.

4. Don't let your faith work be in vain. You have suffered and gone through so much for the Good News of the Gospel to relinquish your authority over again to Satan the devil. Don't throw it away; repent and trust in the Lord with all your heart and lean not to thy own understanding but in all your ways, recognize the Lord and God will direct your ways. Wonderful Jesus!

5. Paul asks the question again, trying to jar and shake their conscience, asking, was it God who gave them the Holy Spirit and the works of miracles because you obeyed the laws of Moses? Definitely not! It was because you believe the word you heard about Jesus, as the Christ through faith, just like Father Abraham believed God. When Paul asked the Galatians in the first century, "Who had bewitched you? Who has cast a spell and bound you, or who has beguiled you? Who is it that hoodwinked you by pulling the wool hood over your eyes and got you to believe something different from the doctrine I have been teaching you about our Lord Jesus the Christ King?"

Paul continued to encourage and advise the Galatians to keep their faith in Christ; he also spoke in the book of 1 Timothy 1:3–4, "As I urged you when I went into Macedonia-remain in Ephesus that you may charge some that they teach no other doctrine, nor give heed to fables and endless genealogies, which cause disputes rather than godly edification which is in faith." This explains to us in detail how to give up those old wives' tales, the idle talk and gossip of women, fables, legends, and endless genealogies—long list of ancestors, Jewish origin myths, and endless wandering along strange roads leading nowhere, which minister questions and produce arguments rather than building up in our most holy faith. Second Timothy 4:3–4 says, "For the time will come when they will not endure sound doctrine, but according to their own desires, because they have itching ears, they will heap up for themselves teachers; and they will turn their ears away from the truth, and be turned aside to fables." False stories and improbable accounts show the time has arrived; however, today, men and women are being indoctrinated but not with sound, true, or solid rudiment nor righteous teaching. But with the world's doctrines have started piling up preachers, stacking up teachers, and amassing entertainers to tickle their fancy to tell them about humanistic philosophy, the sweet by-and-by enchantment of worldly sophistication. Nevertheless, as children of God and colaborers with our Big Brother Almighty Jesus Christ, there will be much sacrifice and perseverance of the saints. However, we are overcome by the blood of the Lamb, and by the words of our testimony, we are more than conquerors. *Hupernikao*, Greek for "super-victorious." *Hooper* means "exceedingly, over and above," then there's *Nic*, *Nike*, or *Nicolas*, which means "victorious/victory." We're always winning. Win, win, win, win, win in Christ Jesus. People are being very selfish and greedy, boastful and conceited; we are becoming insulting and disobedient to our parents, ungrateful and irreligious; we are unkind, merciless, slanderers, violent, and fierce, hating good, loving the wrong sound like somebody is being spellbound and/or brainwashed, holding to the outward form of religion but rejecting the power thereof brainwashed. Are you a Jesus fanatic (bloodwashed) or a religious fanatic (brainwashed)? A Jesus fanatic will die for what he believes, but a religious fanatic will kill for his belief. I' m closing the chapter, but I would like to leave you with this resonating thought.

Are you:

- God the Father led—bloodwashed—or Satan the devil led—brainwashed?
- Jesus Christ led—bloodwashed—or world led—brainwashed?

- The Word led—bloodwashed—or people lad—brainwashed?
- Faith led—bloodwashed—or sight led—brainwashed?
- Love led—bloodwashed—or lust led—brainwashed?
- Charity led—bloodwashed—or money led—brainwashed?
- Steadfastly led—bloodwashed—or unstably led—brainwashed?
- Wisdom led—bloodwashed—or foolish led—brainwashed?
- Spiritual led—bloodwashed—or flesh led—brainwashed?
- Joy led—bloodwashed—or fear led—brainwashed?
- Order led—bloodwashed—or confusion led—brainwashed?
- Hope led—bloodwashed—or chance led—brainwashed?

I am washed in the blood of the Lamb. I am bloodwashed by the Lamb of God, and the blood has miraculous powers! I know it was the blood; I know it was the blood! It was my Savior's blood.

Here are a bunch of bloodwashed questions asked by the writer Elisha A. Hoffman.

Have you been to Jesus for the cleaning power? Are you washed in the blood of the Lamb? Are you fully trusting in his grace this hour? Are you washed in the blood of the Lamb? Are you washed in the blood in the soul cleansing blood of the Lamb? Are your garments spotless? Are they white as snow? Are you washed in the blood of the Lamb? Are you walking daily by the Savior's side? Are you washed in the blood of the Lamb? Do you rest each moment in the crucifixion? Are you washed in the blood of the Lamb? When the Bridegroom cometh will your robes be white? Are you washed in the blood of the Lamb? Will your soul be ready for the mansions bright and be washed in the blood of the Lamb? Lay aside the garments that are stained with sin and be washed in the blood of the Lamb; There a fountain for the soul unclean, O be washed in the blood of the Lamb!

May the God of peace bless you real good!

CHAPTER 8

Slave or Rebel
Jeremiah 27:1–28:17

The question is posted: are you a slave or a rebel? Many people are perplexed at the contrast of the option, for the contrast leaves us wanting both. To be a rebel on one hand and a slave on the other hand is a complex dilemma; however, we must choose one. Some people say and pick slave but most pick and say rebel and then there are a few of those who say both. A slave to serve the will of God the Father and a rebel to revolt against Satan the devil, but that cannot be so. The problem with that is Lucifer, Satan, the devil, is the progenitor of all rebellion and reprobates. We don't have to rebel against Satan, for he has not been given the power or the authority over us; nevertheless, we must stand firm by resisting him with the words of our testimony and by the blood of the Lamb, and he will run away from us. We put Satan to fight, for he is a nuisance and a menace. We have been given the victory and the authority over him through our Lord Jesus, the Anointed King of Glory. You only can rebel or be rebellious against authorized authority ordained by the God of the universe, figures like God Himself, His commandments, government-kingdoms, parents: father and mother, and spiritual leaders. Satan, Lucifer, the devil, was not and is not authorized to rule over the children or the creation of God. Angels and the nine ranking orders were created and ordered to minister/serve God and His offspring, along with creation. We are created and designed to serve and worship God the Father of our Lord and Savior Jesus Christ.

Tony Evens states in his book *Free at Last*, "Freedom is an elusive thing. It's the proverbial carrot on the end of the stick that causes a lot of us mule-headed people to do the things we do." Jesus spoke of freedom, but He spoke of a different kind of freedom: the type of freedom that comes not through power, but through willing submission to a higher power; not through control, but through surrendering your independence to be dependent on a greater authority. Not through wealth or possession, but through open giving. First Peter 2:16–18 tells us to live as free people; do not, however, use your freedom-liberty to cover up any sin, but live as servants of God's slaves. Respect everyone, love others, honor God, and respect the emperor/king/ruler. We as servants/slaves must submit ourselves to our master and show him complete respect, not only to those who are kind and considerate but also to those who are harsh. First Peter 5:5–6 says, "In the same way you young people must submit themselves to their Elders, and all of us must put on the apron of humility to serve one another; for God ordained slavery and its radical humbling concept; and the scripture says God resists the proud but shows favor to the Humble, Humble yourselves then under the mighty hand of God. So that He will lift you up in His own good time."

This here is an awesome text. God the Almighty Father has full and total control over everything and everyone. He is God, sovereign in both heaven and earth, kings and kingdoms, animals and fowls all are in His hand. God the Father is an awesome wonder to perform. Here we see God in His unpredictable ways. He states in the book of 1 Corinthians 1:25–29, "Because the foolishness of God is wiser than men, and the weakness of God is stronger than men. For you see your calling, brethren, that not many wise according to the flesh, not many mighty, not many noble, are called, but God has chosen the foolish thing of the world to put to shame the wise, and God has chosen the weak thing of the world to put to shame the things which are mighty; and the base things of the world and the thing which are despised God has chosen, and the things which are not, to bring to nothing the things that are, that no Flesh should glory in His presence."

There is absolutely no foolishness in God nor is there any in Christ, who is the personification of wisdom; however, Paul maintains and elaborates this contrast that worldly men think spiritual things are foolish. The Jews who look for signs to prove and to see if God is true and real, then there are the Greeks who love wisdom that comes through philosophers, but with their speculation, could not accept the doctrine of salvation based on what they call the foolishness of the cross and of the crucified Jesus of Nazareth.

Man and his wisdom will be destroyed with all of his skepticism and his antagonism of God's word and supreme way of the cross of Christ. God works most wisely and most powerfully in ways directly opposite to human expectations. The human wisdom Paul opposes is not intellect or education, but a false independence of God and a proclivity toward self-sufficiency. God rejects human wisdom because of its pride and self-glory.

Now let's look at the text that pushed my mind off the edge that had me saying, "Wow, look at God and His providential intervention for we live, move, and have our being in Christ Jesus." From the book of Jeremiah chapters 27 and 28, you will discover the connection with the previous paragraph of 1 Corinthians 1:25–29, "Brethren that not many wise in the flesh are called, not many mighty are called, and not many noble are called. But God has chosen the foolish things of the world to put to shame the wise, God has chosen the weak things of the world to put to shame the things which are mighty; and the base things and things which are despised God has chosen."

God chose Abraham out of a pagan family to be the father of the faithful all over the world; God chose Lot to move him out of the region to escape the destruction of Sodom and Gomorrah. God chose Jacob the trickster and changed his name to Israel, the chosen people, and God chose Jacob's sixth son Judah to go first before the people with praise in Israel instead of the firstborn son, Reuben. God chose Joseph, the hated younger brother, to save Israel from a famine to live in Egypt. God chose Benjamin, the baby of the family and the smallest tribe of Israel, and selected Saul, Israel's first king. God chooses despised, weak, and lowly, meek things to confound the mighty, the wise, and the noble. God still operates and uses the shame to get His message and work completed human vessels like King David who went from a shepherd to the king of Israel. A shepherd is one of the most despised and degrading jobs a man could have, but shame builds godly character. I can go on and on and on with the lives God have ordained for His humbling service, but I will end the litany of people God has chosen and go straight to His Son Jesus the Christ, the climax, the peak, the pinnacle, and the high point of God's ultimate plan. Through the obscure Nazarene-born Virgin Mary, the mother of Jesus, Jesus born in an ox stall, laid in a manger, and wrapped in rags in a Roman-occupied Israel in slavery under the oppressions of Augustus Caesar. Jesus then serves as the anointed King of Glory to take away the sins of the world by becoming the sacrificial Lamb of God by saving the world from hell's fire through the foolishness of preaching the parallel and horizontal cross that is love.

Jeremiah is chosen by God to become an object lesson of a debased and despised thing. God told Jeremiah, the weeping prophet, to make a yoke of wood and bond himself as a slave to show the surrounding nations as well as Israel that God will put them under bondage and yoke to humble them for service under the heathen king of Babylon, King Nebuchadnezzar. The king was also used as a servant of God, just as was Pharaoh in Egypt, for God's purpose and glory. God decrees through Jeremiah to Israel and the surrounding nations that they will serve King Nebuchadnezzar or they will be utterly destroyed as God's command. Now rebellious Hananiah, the prophet, prophesied a lie and took the yoke from Jeremiah's neck and broke it, saying, "The Lord will break the yoke of Babylon in two years."

Jeremiah was told by God to go back to Hananiah and tell him that he had broken the yokes of wood, "But I God will replace it with a yoke of iron. The Lord God did not call you, and you are making these people believe a lie. So the Lord Himself says that He is going to get rid of you before this year is over. You will die because you have told the people to rebel against the Lord," and Hananiah died in the seventh month of that same year.

A slave is one that surrenders his entire will over to someone or something, preferably the Lord thy God to serve totally, absolutely. A rebel is just the opposite; he/she is a person who thrives to be disobedient and self-willed, arrogant, proud, and rebellious against authority and God is its author. Rejecting the Lord's commandments by rebellion is as bad as witchcraft. What is witchcraft? *Kashaph* and *qesem* are Hebrew words for those that practice in the league with evil spirits. *Kashaph* is sorcery and *qesem* is divination, but in Greek, divination is *pharmakeia*. Our translation is pharmaceutical/pharmacy; it derives from the use of drugs, charms, magic, and familiar spirits like the woman King Saul looked to find in 1 Samuel 28:7–25 dealing in mediums. All such practices are strictly condemned. Stubbornness, pigheadedness, and mulishness permeates our society by rejecting God's authority and His word. Rebellion witchcraft is ordained and insisted just like the lie Satan authored. Iniquity (vice, wickedness, evil, and sin) and idolatry worshiped everything but the God of the universe, Yeshua Hamashiach. I ask you again, which are you slave or rebel?

The contrast:

Jeremiah was a slave; Hananiah was a rebel.
Jeremiah was a hearer of the Word of God; Hananiah ignored the word of God.
Jeremiah was a doer of the Word of God; Hananiah was a complainer of the Word.
Jeremiah was the keeper of the law of God; Hananiah abandoned the law of God.
Jeremiah was a maker of the bond; Hananiah was a breaker of the yoke.
Jeremiah was obedient; Hananiah was disobedient.
Jeremiah was a surrendered slave; Hananiah was rebellious.
Jeremiah was a truth bearer; Hananiah was a liar and a pretender.
Jeremiah submitted and lived; Hananiah's pride caused him to die.

Rebels died in the book of Numbers 16:1–30. Korah and 250 of his rebellious men went against Moses and Aaron, and God made the earth open up and swallowed them up.

Also in the book of 1 Samuel 15:22–23, King Saul rebelled against God, and Saul and Jonathan both died in battle. In 2 Samuel chapter 20, Sheba, the son of Bichri, a troublemaker, and an ancestor to King Saul, rebelled against King David, and Sheba got his head cut off, for rebels die. This is God's vengeance, retribution, punishment, and revenge.

In conclusion, we should emulate, copy, and mimic the behavior of our Lord and Savior by having the same attitude and mindset Jesus had when he gave up his equal nature with God and submitted to the equal form of a man and a slave. Jesus then took on the nature of a servant/a slave. He became like a man and appeared in human likeness. Jesus the Christ humbled and walked the path of obedience all the way to his death, even the death of the cross. Jesus came to serve, to minister, and not to be ministered to, but to wash the feet of those who need cleaning, to heal the sick, and to feed the poor multitude. Most of all, Jesus came to be a substitute for the propitiation for us by dying on that old rugged cross and to redeem man and his kind back to God the Father. That's slave work. He was doing the work of the lowest of servants. True servanthood: by washing dirty feet, Jesus displayed humility for his disciples. The washing of their feet was a direct contrast to their heart condition and attitudes; the disciples were shocked at the condescending humiliation of their Christ, Lord and Master, washing their feet. When Jesus washed his disciples' feet, He informed them then and tells us today that he is giving us an example that we should do as "I have done to you" (John 13:15). We as Jesus's followers must emulate His work by serving one another in the lowliest heart and of mind, building up one another in love, humility, and meekness (Mark 9:35, 10:44). A servant's heart; the Lord promised we will be greatly blessed (John 13:17). When Jesus stooped down to his lowly task and estate (Matthew 20:28), Jesus came not to be served but to serve and to give his life as a ransom for many. The towel and basin foreshadowed His ultimate act of humility and love on the cross. Jesus told His disciples that His suffering was certain: "The Son of Man must suffer many things and be rejected by the elders, the chief priests and the teacher of the law, and he must be killed and on the third day be raised to life" (Luke

9:22–17:25). Note the word *must*: He *must* suffer; He *must* be killed, tortured, and crucified. Jesus suffered severely throughout his trials; it was physical, spiritual, and emotional. "His appearance was so disfigured beyond that of any man and His form so marred beyond human likeness" (Isaiah 52:14). Jesus was the suffering servant specified for our sins. The suffering of Christ was the plan of God for salvation of the world.

> God's children cannot keep on being sinful. His life-giving power lives in them and makes them His children, so they cannot keep on sinning. You can tell God's children from the devil's children, because those who belong to the devil refuse to do right or to love each other. (1 John 3:9–10 CEV DCI)

> From Simon Peter, a servant and an apostle of Jesus Christ. To everyone who shares with us in the privilege of believing that our God and savior Jesus Christ will do what is just and fair. I Pray that God will be kind to you and will let you live in perfect peace! May you keep learning more and more about God and Lord Jesus. We have everything we need to live a life that pleases God. It was all given to us by God's own power, when we learned He had invited us to share in His wonderful goodness. God made great and marvelous promises, so his nature would become part of us. Then we could escape our evil desires and the corrupt influences of this world. (2 Peter 1:1–4 CEV DCI)

A Major Identity Crisis

If Jesus was to ask you, "Who do men say that the Son of Man is?" what would be your response? Could you identify Him or would you go on with the litany of name-calling and titles or would you depend on listening to the Spirit of God to reveal to you who the Lord is: the Christ, the Son of the life-sustaining God. We, in today's world, are depending on the flesh and blood (earthly wisdom and human intellect) to connect us to his identity. Not knowing that our very own identity is divinely inspired, we are the offspring of God the Father and Jesus is our big brother almighty where grace and peace is multiplied through the knowledge of God and of Jesus Christ our Lord. That by these, we are partakers of God's divine nature, having escaped the corruption that is in the world through lust. Thank God for his seed that dwells in us that keep us from sinning because we are the righteous children born of God

If you were to ask who is Muhammad Ali? What would you say? Most would probably say he was a great boxer. Although Ali was a great boxer and may be the greatest boxer to ever live to fight, but is that who Muhammad Ali is? Is that who he is? No, it's not because being a boxer does not tell us really who Ali is, just what he used to do. Do you see the point? Just hold on, I want to paint you a picture: Look! If Muhammad Ali's total identity were wholly in him being a fighter, what would he now be since he has been out of boxing for many years? Would Ali now be a nobody? Did he stop existing the day he stopped and retired from boxing? No, he did not. One of the greatest mistakes we can make is to define ourselves by what we do or did for a living or for an occupation. The problem is that people love to measure one another with a yardstick of prestige. Let two men meet and the first thing they want to know is what you do for a living. Some of us go to great lengths to get the right identity. There are those who resort to plastic surgery to change our looks, some seek out new friends who will keep them in the loop and looking the part, some will even go as far as buying diplomas and degrees to get better-paying jobs and to impress others. Some of our identities are determined by our performance. Actors, athletes, and entertainers have the tendency of tying their identity to their acting and playing days. We see that propensity in Michael Jordan; he kept coming back, why? Because he is the greatest to play the game, so why continue to break retirement? I am glad you ask; because of performance or the lack thereof, one seems to lose one's identity and does not know what to do with themselves believing that their identity is determined by their work and or performance.

Here is a story of a queen of England who was trying to get her young daughter to sit still and behave during a special event. That worked for a while, but the little girl started to move around and wiggle, then again, the queen told her daughter to stop and be still! Nevertheless, nothing worked to keep the daughter quiet until the queen told her daughter, "Young lady, don't you know who you are? You are a princess and the king's daughter. Act like it."

The little girl finally got the message that time because the queen tied her daughter's behavior to her identity that she is the king's kid. Glory! Hallelujah! For we are the King's kids, His sons, His children if we only knew who you are. The problem is there is confusion of who we are, and we are experiencing a major identity crisis. Once you are confused about your identity, you want to know what to stop doing or what to start doing. It is possible to get people to conform on the outside without change on the inside. However, it will not last. Some of us still want to follow the old ways; we just don't want anyone to know how carnal and fleshly we are. So we sin in private and wear a mask of spiritual religion in public.

CHAPTER 9

The Conflict in Us!
Romans 7:1–25, 8:2

Christians, your body with its fleshly nature is not saved, but it is a slave. From Hebrew *'ebed* (5650) and in Greek, *doulos-soma* (4983), "a body," to be worked, controlled, and manipulated to do the will of God the Father. There is, however, a conflict within us, the human race. Man and his kind, for we are a composition of complex elements: the spirit, the soul, and the body—three in one. In this epistle, you will discover that Paul gives us a graphic description of the tension between our spiritual self and our sinful flesh, our souls and our bodies. We love the law of God, but we lack the ability to keep it. Our attempt is to keep the word of God and too uncomplicate the conflict in us, the tension between the law of God in our mind and the law of sin and death in the flesh. The law is spiritual, but the flesh-body is tainted by sin and has become unspiritual. Consequently, there is nothing good in the flesh-body for the flesh is *basar* and *she'er* in Hebrew and *sarx* in Greek, meaning the physical part of the body is human nature, deprived of the Holy Spirit and dominated by sin. This is why flesh and blood cannot inherit the kingdom of God nor does corruption inherit incorruption (1 Corinthians 15:50).

The body is considered to be mortal and corruptible, not salvageable, but the elements decay the shell but not the seed. Ashes to ashes and dust to dust. Nevertheless, Paul speaks of living with a divided nature: a self that wants to do right and obey the law of God, and another self wanting to do wrong by disobeying the law of God. The question is who is responsible for this tension? Well, naturally, you would think Satan the devil, without a doubt, the tempter; however, we as God's offspring had a choice, and we choose to disobey the will of God the Father, and now we are locked in a law. It's called the law of sin and death that now dwells in our carnal bodies. The letter of the law kills, but the spirit of God makes it alive. Because both good and bad dwell in us as believers in Christ, the good of the believer, which is the law of our mind; the inner man, the spiritual man, delights in the law of the Lord. However, the law of sin and death is in constant opposition to the law of our mind we have in God. This conflict creates a tension that holds us captive and pulls us downward toward the things we do not want to do. To God be the glory for Christ Jesus has saved us from the bondage to sin and death; we are to live as servants/slaves to God in Christ Jesus in love and not live a life of sin, serving as slaves to our fleshly desires. Paul yearned for provision that we should cry to the Lord God and thank Him for a deliverer of our souls, the Lord Jesus Christ. Paul concludes that he is a slave to God's law in that he longs to keep it, but that in his sinful nature, he is also a slave to the law of sin and death because he cannot keep the law. We cannot stop it, but as believers of our Lord and Savior Jesus Christ, we must not live in sin, but we must live in the freedom of the indwelling of the Holy Spirit, which brings tremendous benefits to the lover of the law of God through Jesus Christ. With this revelation from God through slavery, obedience, submission, humility, meekness, and perseverance, we can control the conflict in our bodies to serve the Lord Jesus.

Now let us look at the spirit of man for the spirit is life, breath, wind, and air, and it is invisible. The genesis of it all is that God is a spirit (John 4:24), and in the book of Genesis 1:2, it says, "And the spirit of God moved upon the face of the water" with creative power, force, and authority. The spirit of life comes from God the Father, from God the Son, and from God the Holy Ghost. Therefore, we are quickened by the Spirit and made alive in God, and God said, "Let us make man in our image after our likeness" (Genesis 1:26–27). The words *us* and *our* refer to the three that bear the record in heaven: the Father, the Word, and the Holy Ghost; these three are one, and God counseled no one but Himself, the trinity of the Godhead: God the Father, God the Son, and God the Holy Ghost working as one in union. Jesus the Christ, being the fullness and the personification of the Godhead bodily in the flesh, the Word of God, needed an earthen vessel of flesh and blood, a body of sin to submit for sacrifice on the altar of that old rugged cross of Calvary to die for the sins of the world. The virgin birth was necessary for our understanding of the incarnation of the Word of God taking on the body of flesh. The process of ordinary birth is a new personality being born; however, Jesus Christ did not begin to be at birth. He is and will always be the eternal son of God, the Word of God from the beginning. The virgin birth was a miracle of God's wisdom and the Holy Ghost. Jesus was not half man nor is he half god like the mythology of Greek heroes, but Jesus is fully God and fully man, genuine divinity and humanity. However, now, He has a glorified body with the marks and scars of his crucifixion. The tangible nature of the body of the resurrected Lord, the risen Jesus, has a body of flesh and bones but not of blood; he was not a ghost nor a vapor, but a body that could eat food. The resurrected body will be our very own body. It was Jesus's own body, sown a natural man, and raised a spiritual body as the eternal son of God in the flesh; Jesus existed before his manifestation in time. He was and is the word of life. Jesus has God the Father's full nature. He is the Word that became flesh and dwelt among us, and we beheld His glory, the magnificence as of the only begotten of the Father, full of grace and truth. Jesus is the archetype and the model in which man was made. He is the last Adam (1 Corinthians 15:45).

Genesis 1:27 continues to say, "So God created man in his own image." In the image of God, He created male and female and created Adam. Genesis 2:7 says, "And the Lord God formed man of the dust of the ground and breathed into his nostrils the breath-spirit of life and man became a living soul." Simply, the spirit of man is the candle of the Lord, and the spirit of God is in the nostrils, the life-giving source, so we see a man going the way of the Lord, how can a man then understand our own ways? The spirit comes from

God, the spirit is God's, and the spirit goes right back to God. The spirit is eternal and will live forever in an appointed place whether heaven or hell in the lake of fire. After the breath-spirit of God is blown into the nostrils of the formed dust man, man became a living soul, a *nephesh*, a Hebrew word meaning "vitality, living, breathing, thinking, feeling, seeing, hearing, learning, working, walking, talking, and worshiping being." Very much an animated character, a Pinocchio of sorts.

The second component of the animated human being is his soul, *nephesh*. The soul is an awesome thing; it is the heart and center of all human imagination, emotion, will, intellect, attitude, and mind. The soul is influenced by knowledge, information, and wisdom, primarily and preferably from God. The Holy Spirit is the spirit of truth, the leader to all truth, all reality, all accuracy, and all legitimacy; the Spirit of God will show us things to come through vision and revelation. God's Word is good and is the creative force given to the soul of man to possess great authority and dominion over every living thing upon the earth; nevertheless, the soul of man has an opposition, and it is Satan and this world of sight, lust, and pride. However, Hebrews 4:12 gives us assurance and confidence in God and His Word. Jesus the Christ that we operated in the spirit of meekness, which is power under control.

"For the word of God is quick, and powerful, and sharper than any two edged sword, piercing even to the dividing asunder of soul and spirit, and of the joints and marrow, and is a discerner of the thoughts and intents of the heart." The Word of God is life; it quickens the lifeless and prevails triumphantly over everything against the Word of God; the Word also cuts microscopic razor thin, separating the spirit of man and the breath of God and the blood of man. The Word of God recognizes and detects truth and lies, also the very intentions, thoughts, and imagination of the heart of man and his kind. The heart is the part of an individual where character is developed, and apart from God, one's heart and soul is deceitful and desperately wicked (Jeremiah 17:9–10). God searches the minds and tests the hearts of people, and He treats each of them according to the way they live, according to what they do. In conclusion, we are to love the Lord God with all our heart, with all our soul, and with our entire mind and all of our strength; all of these deal with the personality of man. Believers must get the Word of God in their hearts, for with the heart, man believes unto righteousness; we are made right with God, and with the mouth, confession is made unto salvation. You are saved forever!

The final component of the human being is the body (Greek *soma*). The word has a wide range of meanings in Matthew 27:52. It can refer to a corpse; in Mark 5:29, it refers to one's physical body, and the human self expressed in and through the body. Is the body of death the container, the shell, and the Bible calls it an earthen vessel? It embodies the spirit and the soul of man. Nevertheless, the body of this death is sinful; it's weak, it's ugly, and it's mortal and must be controlled, discipled, dominated, and enslaved to operate in its full pretense. Death is loss and separation; loss and separation is categorically opposite to God's character. God is all about gain, increase, and multiplication. God is a winner; all He does is win, win, win no matter what. God is victorious in death and loss, exceedingly victorious (*hoopernikiao*, super victorious). No fear is in God for God has not given us the spirit of fear but of love, power, and a sound mind. Fear is an exceptional verb that has a dual concept: the word *fear* in Greek means "phobia, fright, dread, or revere," and we have an innate physical need of fear: to fight or flight, to respect clear, apparent, and present danger. It is intrinsic that the fleshly body fears God the Father of our Lord and Savior Jesus Christ, to revere Him, to worship Him, and to respect Him. Nevertheless, God did not give His children the spirit-life existence to fear anything outside Himself. God is a Spirit, and those who worship Him must fear Him, must respect Him, must revere Him. In spirit and in truth, God is to be gloried and hailed in high esteem.

Death is our last and greatest enemy. The conflict is that we do not understand what we do as human beings. We do not do what we would like to do, but instead, we do what we hate. Since what we do is what we do not want to do, this shows that we agree that the law is right. So we are not really the ones who operate this thing, rather it is the sin that lives in us. We know that good does not live in us;

that is in our bodies. Even though the desire to do good is in us, we are not able to do it. We don't do the good we want to do; instead, we do the evil that we don't want to do. The meaning of this is that we are no longer the one who does it; instead, it is sin that lives in our mortal bodies. We find that this law is at work when we want to do what is good; what is evil is the only choice we have. Our inner being delights in the law of God, but we see a different law at work in our body members. A law that fights against the law, which our mind approves of, makes us a prisoner to the law of sin, which is at work in our bodies. Our condition is this: we can serve God's law only with our minds while our flesh serves the law of sin. Oh, miserable and dejected people that we are, who will rescue and deliver us from the bodies that are taking us to this death? Thanks be to God who gives us the victory through our Lord and Savior Jesus Christ. There is now therefore no condemnation to those who live in union with Christ Jesus, who has made us free from the law of sin and death. The body is sin, but the law is spiritual. We are carnal goods sold as slaves to sin, shapened in iniquity, and in sin did our mothers conceive us. Those who live as their flesh nature tells them to have their minds controlled by what the body of death wants; those who live as the spirit tells them to are controlled by the Holy Spirit. First Peter 2:11 informs us not to give into bodily passions, which are always at work against the soul. The flesh and the soul are enemies, and this means that you cannot do what you want to do. If the spirit leads you, then you are not subject to the law of sin. The body shows itself as an immoral, filthy, and indecent act, like idol worship, witchcraft, hatred, jealousy, adultery, fornication, wrath, strife, ambitions, and other wicked things. Get rid of every filthy habit and all wicked conduct in the name of Jesus! Submit yourself to God, and accept the word that He plants in your hearts and souls, which is able to save you from eternal death. Put off the body of sin of the flesh by the cutting, cleaning, and purging of filth out of our hearts and souls when we first believe. He freed us from the power of this sinful flesh. The body will die and be buried, planted like a seed mortal, and will be raised good and immortal. When the body is buried, it is ugly and weak; raised, it will be beautiful and strong. When buried, it is corruptible; when raised, it is incorruptible. When buried, it is a physical body; when raised, it is a spiritual body. There is of course a physical body, so there has to be a spiritual body. The scriptures say the first man Adam was created a living being, but the last man Adam (Jesus) is the life-giving spirit. We need to ask God Almighty to create in us a clean heart and to renew a truthful spirit within us. So that we can present our bodies as a living sacrifice, holy and up to God's standard, which is our logical and enthusiastic worship. This is the true service of the servant slave that we should no longer be conformed to this worldly system, but that our minds changed and renewed in us. That we may prove what is that good and satisfactory, wonderful will of God!

Free from the Law of Sin and Death

For the law of the spirit of life in Christ Jesus
hath made us free from the law of sin and death.
(Romans 8:2)

There is a doctrine of the law of sin and death (Romans 5:12–21). Death in Adam, life in Jesus.

Hamartiology is a doctrine of sin; it is the principal teaching of the sin and death law, sin being a unique law, saying the wages of sin is death (Romans 6:23). Therefore, sin is positively and absolutely evil and is not a lesser degree of good; sin is not only unlike God in its character, it is also actively opposed to God and His will. Hamartiology defines sin as missing the mark by err, offense, guilt, forfeit, lack, and through trespassing, falling short of God's glory. Sin is a force that rules and impels angels to feel and sin as well as man and his kind. Evil is the root of sin and expresses itself in the behavior of falling angels and falling humanity. There are three categories of sin: the origin of sin, original sin, and actual sin. The origin of sin is in relationship with Lucifer's fall and Satan—the pride, the arrogance, and the lie. According to Isaiah 14:12–14 and Ezekiel 36, evil was here before man and his kind came on the scene. Thank God that sin is not eternal; it has a definite beginning and a definite end (Revelations 20:1–10). The law of sin and death troubles every human being on earth, for the last enemy to be destroyed is sin and death. The saved and the unsaved person's sins take up residence in the body of death; that is the sin industry. The law of sin and death completely dominates the lives of the unsaved person to the extent that they are forever enslaved by sin, the producer of death. Despite the relatively good things that they do, their whole bent of life is toward sinning and the total output of their lives consists only of sin *in* God's sight (Roman 3:10–12). The unsaved have neither the will nor the ability to do what is right before God and yet every saved believer on earth still has the same sin law within his bodily flesh. This accounts for those inner evil urges that we sometimes feel; however, because of the radical changes that salvation had brought us through Jesus Christ we have made in our lives, we no longer sin in a continuous state as unsaved people do (1 John 3:4–10). We now commit acts of sin and acts of righteousness according to the dominating moral force in us—God or sin—that is in command of our hearts. Man, in his own nature, is sinful, and we are not at all reluctant prisoners. We actually love to sin and evil; we love sin to death. In each of us, there is sin. We are not just susceptible to sin; sin is in us. It is more than a weakness; we sin for the sake of sinning.

Why do we find sin so alluring? There's a dark side that passes right through every one of our hearts. We love the world, the flesh, and the pride of life. Is there anything else that would explain hunger for war, mayhem, and our secret pleasure in someone's fall? We also have a morbid attraction with TV violence, blood, and the murders in terror movies. We even avoid our own responsibilities and then blame Satan for everything we can imagine. We even omit things which are an act of sin and our commission is sin. Sin is not hypothetical; it is not a theory or an idea scientists use to discuss nor is sin honorary as a degree given. Neither is sin vicariously lived through the experience of others. We sin in reality and in activities; most of us go through life without bearing in mind our personal sin and shame publicized all over the news, media headlines, billboards, and the social network. Our indiscretion mostly remains our own secret baggage. I must say truly, there is a line that separates good and evil, and it goes right through every one of our human hearts. This is where the real war is being waged and fought. This war is not between good people and bad people, it is not between sinner and saint, it is not between Jew and gentile, nor is it between Catholic and Protestant; neither is it being waged for mere national or international stakes. The war to end all wars is a battle for eternal interest and involvement between the spiritual forces, between God the Creator, the Father of universal love and truth, and Lucifer, the devil, Satan, the liar, the curse of the brethren, and the deceiver. This war is being waged in the hearts of men and women all over the world, in you and me; sin expresses itself in a myriad of sinful activities, in words, actions, thoughts, ideas, subjections, wills, emotions, attitudes, intents, and in our motives; but these activities are not the root of sin, they are the fruit of sin. Without a vessel or an instrument of expression, this evil force could not manifest itself by these evil works. We are the vessels, the musical instruments that are being played by faith in God or by sin, but when we yield to God's control and His obedience, He expresses Himself through us in the melodious sound of music of the spirit of life and the beauty of holiness. However, when Satan and sin have control over our lives, it is only expressed in our bad and evil behavior; it becomes the discord of the noise of sinful activities, the moral depravity, and spiritual and physical death!

However, there is a great problem with our grammar and syntax of the word *sin*, and it is with verbs and nouns. You see, *sin* is a noun, and nouns are used in sentences as a person, a place, or a thing; *sin* is not a verb because verbs merely show or explain things away and give excuses of things we do. For example, when I lie, this is a verb that explains what I did: I lied. However, it is a lot different from admitting that I am a liar or to say I am a thief (a noun)! This just says we are controlled by the law of sin, for the law of sin rules over man and his kind as long as we are alive in the body of this sin. As far as the law is concerned, we, the saved, the believers in Christ Jesus, are dead to the law of sin and death, being baptized in the body of Christ. We are to mortify the deeds of our bodies, put the thoughts, ideas, and subjections to death, pull down every imagination that exhorts itself against God the Father's authority. We must simply die before we die, for when we die, we want to die. God has made a way for us to be free from the evil law of sin and death through the door and blood of Jesus Christ our Lord and the repentance of our sins. Confessing our sins unto God, for God is faithful and just to forgive us and to cleanse us from all unrighteousness (Romans 8:917; 1 John 1:9). For this purpose, the Son of Man was manifested that he might destroy the works of sin and the devil. There is now therefore no conviction to them, which are in Christ Jesus, who walk not after the flesh but after the spirit, for the law of life in Christ hath made us free from the law of sin and death. For where sin abound, grace much more abound! We either die to sin or die in sin! Death is the only alternative; it's our transition, our separation, our loss that must happen. Jesus died for us, but we must die from us, from the deeds of the flesh, to show our true love and gratitude to our Lord and Savior Jesus Christ, who became sin for us and paid it all by nailing all our sin and shame to the cross.

CHAPTER 10

Brought with a Price
1 Corinthians 6:18–20

Flee fornication. Every sin that a man doeth is without the body; but he that committeth fornication sinneth against his own body. What! Know ye not that your body is the temple of the Holy Ghost which is in you, which ye have of God, and ye are not your own? For ye are bought with a price; therefore, glorify God in your body, and in your spirit which are God's.

Paul calls on the Corinthian Christians of the first century as well as Christendom in the twenty-first century to flee from fornication as well as all forms of sexual immorality, for its etymology comes from the Hebrews word *zanah* (2181), which means "whoredom," and *taznuwth-taznuth* (8457) "idolatry," and the Greek word *porneia* (4203) which comes from the word *pornography* and *harlotry*. Fornication leads to bondage, and it also opens doors to seducing spirits (1 Timothy 4:1). The Greek word for "seducing spirits" is *planos*, which means "to wander and to stray like a roaming vagabond." It pulls a person away from the truth of God. The best way to deal with *porneia* and *taznuth* is to flee from it! I mean to literally run away. Some things are too powerful to be opposed, so safety only comes in flight and by avoiding all sexual temptations. We have seen and heard of the many great men and even women who have get caught in the clutches of Porneia's crafty and enticing words by trying to interview and have dialogue with sexual active fornicators and have been led astray down to the pit of hell and death (Proverbs 5:1–8, 7:25–27).

Paul continually reminds us by pointing out that fornication is a sin that will affect our own bodies. Paul saw the body not merely as an outer shell to house the spirit and soul, but as the expression of the whole person (Romans 12:1). Therefore, Paul warns against the misuse of the body especially since it is the temple of the Holy Spirit; in the case of the believer, the body is affected by sin and so may be called "the body of sin" (Romans 6:6) and the "body of death" (7:24), which is the nature of the flesh. Even so, Paul's use of the word "body" that must be distinguished from his use of the word "flesh" has always pointed to the principle of sin rampant in human nature and in our bodies. Nevertheless, all other sins affect the outward bodies and all of those we sin against and trespass, but fornication is uniquely different for fornicators; it is that their sin is against the very nature and purpose of their bodies; its effect brings violence and condemnation against their own bodies. Sex, however, is a beautiful and a wonderful gift from God. It is the method God uses for human's procreation, and fruitful sex is technically a blood transmission between a man and a woman in holy matrimony, bonding two individuals together as one flesh ordained of God. Sex is used to unite the man and his wife together as two becoming one flesh. This is the spiritual work of God and it is a mystery, but it concerns Christ and the church for we are members of Christ's body, of his flesh, and of his bones. For this cause shall a man leave his father and mother and shall be joined unto his wife as one flesh. Sex is just as much spiritual as it is physical, for it is a form of worship, love, and adoration unto God. If you were to pay close attention and listen to the utterances that were made doing your intimate activity, you will discover that praise and worship is going on with a lot of "Thank You, Jesus." It is as if we have entered into the holy of holies to worship God Almighty. For the blood and the DNA in the semen is who you are as a man entering the woman and exchanging bodily fluids through intercourse must produce life and responsibility, and that is awesome! Nonetheless, fornicators create a world of uncertainty and a messy situation for life because the sexual relationships are illegitimate and produce bastard children that will affect one's life forever. Furthermore, there will always be imagery of the persons out of our past that will involuntarily pop up at the most unusual times in your consciences, the seed of our sowing.

We as Christians and as the children of the Most High God, being Christlike, the anointed men, women, boys, and girls have been set free from the law of sin and death, for we are dead to sin (Romans 6:7), and we will no longer allow anything to master us again. Christian freedoms do not make us a slave to our desires and instincts, but we are to master them. We are not free to sin, but free not to sin; we are dead-to-sin servants of the Lord Jesus Christ. The Holy Spirit insists that we are not our own, but that we are bought with a price, purchased by Christ: redeemed. Saints, each one of us, have been given the privilege of being the temple of the Holy Spirit, so immoral behavior desecrates the temple of God. Believers need to remember that we belong to Christ, since Jesus paid for our lives with his very own blood. That holy blood redeemed us both body and soul, and now we must give God all the honor and glory He so rightly deserves with our bodies as the building of worship. We must present our bodies as a living sacrifice, holy, acceptable unto God, which is our reasonable, logical, practical, and sensible service and worship (Romans 12:1b). Being redeemed by the blood of Christ Jesus, we are now the bodies and the temples of the Holy Spirit; this brings us into a sharp contrast with the Christian concept of holiness with that of the pagans in Corinth. Wherein the temple of Aphrodite, the Greek goddess of love and beauty, their prostitutes were priestesses having intercourse with whom they counted as dedication to the temple. The Greek temple is *naos*, and God's temple is *naos, hieron,* the name given to the complex of buildings in Jerusalem that was the center of the sacrificial ritual for the Hebrews—at least in Old Testament times. By the time of Christ, the importance of the temple was somewhat lessened because of the place of the local synagogue in Jewish life. The naos is the building that contains the holy place and the holy of holies, and the hieron comprises the whole temple area. Here, the local church is referred to, but 1 Corinthians 6:19 application is to the individual believers as *naos*. The Holy Spirit is the seal of God's purchase having the imagery of the slave-market trade and the exchange of ownership (1 Peter 1:18, 19).

The body is not self-governing or self-sustaining; the Holy Spirit lives in the believer's body, but sin and shame lives in the unbeliever's body. The believer cannot claim ownership, just stewardship. We own nothing; we are just leasing temporarily for a season. And as we maintain our lease, we have the authority and the responsibility to let our light shine before men and women of the world so that they may see our good work, as we reflect that light back to God our Father which art in heaven. The Greeks were inclined to despise the human body. One of their proverbs stated, "The body is a tomb," and the Stoic philosopher Epictetus said, "I am a poor soul shackled to a corpse." This has some reality, but the attitude produced two different ways of treating the body. Some Greeks adopted a scrupulous ruggedness in an attempt to control the body and humiliate its desires and instincts. I agree somewhat with this premise of humiliation, meekness, and self-control, for the Bible encourages us to purge ourselves; it even tells us to mortify the deeds of the body that we may live. Jesus Himself took on the body of flesh as a manservant and humbled Himself and became obedient unto death, even the death of the cross. This is our example and like-mindedness that we have the same love, being of one accord; let nothing be done through strife or vainglory, which is excessive pride and boasting about personal achievements that have become an epidemic in our society. But God recommends that we be in the lowliness of heart and let each esteem others better than themselves; this will kill the instincts to be selfish. We are not to look every man on his own things, but every man on the things of others (Philippians 2:1–7). Then there are others who argued that since the body was worthless and only the spirit was important, it did not matter what they did in and to the body; clearly, the Corinthians were inclined to this view. They felt free to indulge their bodily desires, arguing from the analogy that food is intended for the stomach and the stomach is intended for food, meaning lust as much as you could consume. Paul reminds them in the first century and us today in the twenty-first century that the body is not meant for sexual immorality, but for the Lord. Christians belong to Christ both physically and spiritually. Believers make up the body of Christ here on earth, and our physical bodies are as much part of his body as our souls. So when we indulge in sexual immorality, it is as if we are making the body of Christ commit fornication! Paul quotes Genesis 2:24 to remind us that sexual intercourse creates a union; like glue that binds people together, we are glued to Christ and not to prostitutes. However, the book of Hosea shows another side of this complete mystery though.

A Wife for Sale, I Bought the Whore Back!
Hosea 1:2–3

To be bought means that someone possessed something and had it up for sale or for the best offer that was too hard to refuse, and it was a purchase obtained, acquired, and procured at a firm cost. God bought and purchased the world by the blood of His only begotten son, full of grace and truth. He procured us for the exorbitant price of the life of his darling, perfect son, Jesus of Nazareth, the Lamb of God. But only to those who have received Him as their Lord and Savior, He laid it all down to be exalted.

> The beginning of the word of the Lord by Hosea, and the Lord said unto Hosea. "Go, take unto thee a wife of whoredom and children of whoredom: for the land hath committed great whoredom, departing from the Lord." So he went and took Gomer, the daughter of Diblaim; which conceived, and bore him a son.

God commissioned Hosea, calling him salvation, our deliverance. God chose Hosea to live out His message to the people by being the subject lesson of the unique love of God. The people thought the love of God could be bought back to God. Love never gives up!

The first command Hosea received from the Lord was disturbing. God tells him to go, take to himself an adulterous wife, and not just adultery unfaithfulness, but a whore, prostituting herself throughout the nation. Hosea had to marry potentially the worst kind of woman you could marry, a wife of harlotry. The reason given is that Israel has departed from the Lord, and Gomer was the illustration of the character of the nation Israel which had become a nation of idolatry, just as disloyal and unfaithful to the Lord God by straying away with seducing spirit, "Planos," and Israel has wandered and strayed away from the Lord God of Israel.

Some scholars disagree on the details of Hosea's marriage; some are so shocked and taken aback at the idea of a prophet of God really marrying a prostitute. They insist that He is merely presenting an allegory. Why is it so shocking that God would order Hosea to marry a harlot when, in this case, God himself is married to an unfaithful wife, Israel, who loves worshiping and whoring after other gods; it is a lesson of empathy. Others argue that Gomer cannot have been a prostitute at the time Hosea married her; the view taken here is that, at the time of their wedding, she was a virgin, but later committed adultery and forsook him. Moreover, there are even other positions taken that she was probably already a prostitute at the time of their marriage. I agree with the latter: God telling Hosea to go take a harlot whose father is Diblaim. It is noteworthy that the father mentioned seeing the meaning of his name is dual or two cakes; hence, two faces, two coats, and two covers. Gomer, as well as Israel, lived double lives trying to serve two masters; it is impossible to serve two masters, for you will love one and hate the other or else cling to one and reject the other. No man or woman can serve two masters subsequently Hosea knows what and who she was when he took her home. The problem lay in the unfaithfulness of his wife, Gomer, but Hosea remained faithful to Gomer, even to the extent of buying her back from selling herself into slavery and prostitution. Out of the anguish of his own soul, he understood and appreciated the broken heart of God over the whoredom of Israel, who followed other gods and neglected Him as the Husband, the Creator, and the only Lover of Israel. He was married to a backsliding nation; this adultery recurs repeatedly throughout Hosea's marriage and throughout Israel's biblical history. The book of Hosea was and is still an objective lesson to the children of Israel; they needed to see how awful it looks and appears and the agony it brings to a loving God! This first chapter gives us an account of the recorded word of the Great I Am to the prophet Hosea to go and marry a woman of harlotry and to bear children out of her whoredom. Israel was just as disloyal to God as Gomer was to Hosea; they married and bore three children whose names became a symbol of the situation and condition of Israel. The first son was Jezreel, meaning "God scatters" or "God sows." Jezreel was the name of the place where Jehu had killed seventy sons of Ahab (2 Kings 10:11). As Jehu ended the line of Ahab, therefore, God will bring an end to the whole dynasty of Israel; by 722 BC, the northern kingdom and its capital, Samaria, will fall. Eventually, Jezreel will take on its positive meaning of "God plants." God said he will break the bow of Israel in the valley of Jezreel; breaking the bow in Israel symbolizes breaking Israel's military power. Hosea emphasizes the similar sound of the words Israel (yisra'el) and Jezreel (yizre'el) in the Hebrew tongue. The second child was a daughter, and God told Hosea to name her Lo-Ruhamah, meaning "no mercy," for there would be no mercy on Israel; there will be a lifting of the Lord God's compassion on this rebellious and adulterous nation. God would ordain slavery for the children of Israel. The third child would be a son named Lo-Ammi, meaning "you are not my people," the end of our relationship. The children continued in the sins of their mother in the shameful harlotry, and there will be no mercy for them.

Baal = ba'al pronounced "bah-ahl," literally means "lord or master, also possessor, owner, obtainer, and husband." Because of its use for Canaanite deities, Baal was the god of fertility, and the Israelites were thanking Baal for their harvests of grain and wine and for the growth of their flocks and herds, but in truth, it is God the Father who gives and withholds prosperity and because it implied ownership rather than relationship. God will disassociate Himself from the use of the term and the name Baal, "For I am the one and only living and true God and the Master of the universe therefore, I'll rather be called Ishi or my husband" (Hosea 2:16–17).

God's people hoped for a new day, and God wanted to change his position with His people; He no longer wanted to be identified with Baal as master, implying owner or possessor. Despite the fact God is their master, He is, in essence, love, and He wanted to be called Ishi for affection of relationship. "I will take from your mouth the name Baal and I will betroth you to me forever in righteousness and justice, in loving kindness and mercy, and in faithfulness it shall come to pass." This is the climax of this episode; it is the complete renewal of the covenant relationship as the Lord affirms his betrothal ceremony and how it was much more binding than a mere engagement of today. It was the first step in marriage as a result of God not simply taking back an errant wife, but He is starting the marriage all over again. God's betrothal gift to his beloved bride include righteousness, justice, love, compassion, and faithfulness; these characteristics will define their new relationship. They are the characteristics that God will inspire in and expect from His wife and His people. Hosea indicates that the ideal is for God's people to live in the right relationship with God, with each other, and with the environment. Our relationship with the Lord is not restored because of anything we have done, but primarily through love and the amazing grace of God. Hosea 3:1–5 is Hosea's own account of his personal life and difficulties in marriage to an unfaithful wife.

Abraham Heschel, a Jewish theologian, noted that "to be a prophet was both a distinction and an affection." This was certainly true for Hosea as the Lord commands him to take back and love his unfaithful wife again. Hosea finds his wife on sale at a slave auction, perhaps for a debt, and he bought back Gomer for fifteen pieces of silver and a one and one half of a barrel of barley equivalent to thirty pieces of silver, the price of a slave. This would suggest that Hosea did not possess enough silver to buy Gomer back, but he had to make up the difference by gathering all of his resources. Therefore, Hosea had some requirements before redeeming Gomer back: "You must stay with me for many days. You shall not play the harlot I will be toward you. For the children of Israel shall abide many days without a king or a prince without sacrifice or sacred pillar, without ephod or teraphim."

Hosea paid half of the price in silver and the other half in goods about five bushels of barley. The return to the home or the Presence of God involves a period of discipline; the deprivation of religion is compared to the deprivation of the prophet's wife. This would be particularly significant if she had been compelled to sell herself into slavery because of her infidelities. Applied to Israel, it means simply that persistence in their behavior and in Baalism will bring tragedy and consequences, even exile away from the religious opportunities offered at the sacred shrines. The land would be without all the structures and resources they had depended on for help and guidance. The loss of these things means Israel would be without the mixture of essentials ordained of God for Israel's worship and practices that were forbidden by God, indicating how far the syncretistic people had gone away from God into a synthetic form of worship. For example, the ephod was the part of the high priest's clothing to which the Urim and Thummim were attached. Nevertheless, the teraphim were household gods, probably the images of ancestors. The children of Israel would dwell many days without a king, a prince, a sacrifice pillar, and an ephod or a teraphim. And all the accouterments of the cult, so the reference must be to a period of the lost nationhood. The king and the prince were central figures in the religious practices, and the lack of ritual implement must signify the absence from the place where they could legitimately be used. It is possible that in Hosea's time, they were somehow connected with priestly rites, though absolutely abhorred by earlier and later prophets. The passage suggests that religion as a practice in Hosea's day in Israel will be abolished after a period of purging and education. Israel, the wife, shall repent and return and seek and desire the Lord, her husband and their God. The word *exile* is not mentioned as return, out of exile, in light of his experience of the hand of God in family life and the understanding of the will and purpose of God for his people. Perhaps when the trouble and slavery has come on them or when God's discipline has produced its work, they will come to the Lord trembling with fear and reverence, praying for His goodness and His mercy! Hallelujah!

Even the New Testament writers draw upon Hosea for teaching about the life and ministry of Jesus. Matthew looks into chapter 11:1

of Hosea at the prophecy that was fulfilled when Jesus as a baby was literally taken into and brought out of Egypt parallel to Israel's long stay in Egypt and their Exodus. Jesus fulfills Hosea's promise that one would break the power of death and the grave and bring resurrection, deliverance, and victory. Jesus, in two of his sermons to the Pharisees, takes His text from Hosea. When questioned about His spending time in the home of tax collectors and sinners, Jesus quotes Hosea to show that God desires not just empty words or heartless rituals, but genuine care and concern for people's needs above religious form (Hosea 6:6; Matthew 9:13, 12:7).

Hosea 13:14 and 1 Corinthians 15:55 mentions a ransom from the grave. Paul teaches us that Christ is the groom and the church is the bride, and there is a marriage ceremony and vows where God entered into a permanent relationship with Israel. Hosea 2:19–20 and Ephesians 5:25–32 says, "I will betroth you forever; yea I will betroth thee unto me in righteousness." Hosea was to be a living illustration of God's love for his people. He also calls us to equally demonstrate the same kind of love toward one another with unconditional love. Hosea reveals God's loving heart and God's desire to bless His people to outshine their dark days of sins. Repeatedly, God returns to the promise of restoring relationships as the purpose of His necessary judgment. The Lord our God puts premium value on His relationships with us, so let us seek faithfully to return. That love with obedience and being an extension of any broken relationship asks and looks for opportunities to be an expression of God's love in all we do.

Hosea 5:15 states, "I will go and return to my place till they acknowledge their offense and seek my face in their affection they will seek me early." God withdraws to His place in heaven and leaves Israel to fend for themselves using affliction, hardship, and even slavery, for an earnest and sincere process to get them to repentance, seek His face and to be in His presence again.

God condemns pagan worship in Hosea 4:11, saying, "Harlotry, wine and new wine enslaves the heart of the people and the people ask counsel from their wooden idols and their staff declares unto them for the spirit of whoredom have caused them to err, and they have gone a whoring from under their God." The people of God are robbed of their righteous mind when they drink in excess the old and new wine and are under the spell of idols, delighting in spiritual prostitution, preferring shame rather than honor by continuing to do what pleases them.

Hebrews 12:3–11 says, "Whom the Lord loveth them He chastens and punishes every son whom He receives. If you endure chastening, God deals with you as his sons; for what son is he whom the father chastened not but if you be without chastisement, whereof all are partakers, then are you bastards, and not sons."

Hosea 8:13 says, "They will return to Egypt. Slavery for Israel has forgotten its maker and Ephraim shall return to Egypt's slavery and shall eat the unclean things in Assyria for the scripture says to Pharaoh for this purpose I have raised you up."

God said, "My people are bent on backsliding from me; though they call them to the most high, none at all would exalt him" (Hosea 13:2). They sin more and more, and the people sacrifice unto idols and kiss the molten calves, just like athletes of today that end their season by worshiping their championships and kissing trophies. Kissing the Stanley Cup, kissing the Vince Lombardi football trophies, and kissing the NBA basketball, for they worship with a kiss. Even legalistic religious worshippers kiss the ring of pious men. First Kings 19:18 inform us that his children should not bow down to or kiss idols, yet God said, "I have left for Myself seven thousand men and women in Israel, a remnant that would not bend their knees or bow unto Baal, and every one of their mouth will never kiss Baal."

Take these words with you, and return to the Lord the words of repentance and a continual offering of the sacrifice of praise to God with the fruit of our lips. Who is wise? Who is prudent? Let him know and understand these things, for the way of the Lord is right and the righteous walk in them; to walk is to continue in obedience to God's precepts, but transgressors stumble in them and destruction will come to the worker of iniquity.

The love Hosea had for his rebellious wife is a reminder that God's love is premium and that the spirit of love comes from the fruit of the Spirit and the love of God in our hearts. God's love gives us power to endure all things, even to move mountains. The love of God never fails; this love causes us to change. God loves to outlast our sins and His love outlives the iniquities of us all. God's love will send His only beloved and begotten Son to die for the sins of the world. Glory! Hallelujah! To God be the glory! Thank You, Lord God our Father!

CHAPTER 11

Brotherly Love
Philemon and Onesimus
Master and Slave

Note how Paul starts this letter by telling us that he is a prisoner and a slave of our Lord and Savior Jesus Christ and not of Caesar and the Roman Empire. Paul sees himself through the sight of faith, being incarcerated in a Roman jail physically but in bonds to God and Christ spiritually; in addition, Timothy, Paul's liaison and son in the ministry. To Philemon, their beloved yokefellow and friend, as well to his beloved wife, Apphia, son Archippus, and the church in their home.

This epistle is Paul's personal letter appealing to Brother Philemon on behalf of Brother Onesimus, Philemon's slave who damaged his goods and ran away; mind you, Philemon was a wealthy Christian minister that lived in the town of Colosse and owned slaves. Philemon was converted to Christianity under Apostle Paul's ministry (verse 19), and so was Onesimus (verse 10) who also resided in the city of Colosse where the church met in Philemon's house (verse 2). Paul wrote this epistle during his first time imprisonment in Rome about AD 61. Paul's genuine desire was for a God-style reconciliation between a slave owner who was wronged by a runaway slave named Onesimus who fled to Rome after damaging his master's property. Onesimus came in contact with the imprisoned Paul who led him to Christ. Paul eventfully writes to the church in Colossae and included this letter on behalf of Onesimus to Philemon, and Tychicus, Paul's companion, delivered both letters to the church at Colosse in Philemon's house. The relationship that Paul and Philemon had was very close and is evident by their mutual prayers and an open door of love, trust, respect, hospitality, and friendship.

Slavery was an accepted Roman social reality of that day, and it was a part of their world economics. A slave was his master's property and was without rights under Roman's law, and a runaway slave could be severely punished and even condemned to death for insubordination. Slaves' uprising in the first century resulted in fearful and suspicious owners, while Paul and the early Christian church did not directly attack the institution of slavery. It reordered the relationship between master and slave; both were considered equal before the God of the universe (Galatians 3:38), and both were accountable for their behavior. God's deep providence is his divine care was at work even in Onesimus's initial act of running away. Now, after the conversion of Onesimus, he is now a slave to Christ; there is a new and eternal relationship between master and slave. Onesimus is now a believer of the Lord and Savior Jesus Christ and has become a beloved brother to Philemon in Christ. Now they are no more temporary slave and master in the earthly realm, but eternally, brothers in the spiritual realm. The principles he espouses lay the foundation for future reformation in abolishing slavery and it did.

The epistle to Philemon has become an important text concerning slavery in the new world of America; it was promoted by both sides of the argument: pro-slavery supported it to maintain slavery and the abolitionists to abolish slavery. In this epistle, Paul writes that he is returning Onesimus, a fugitive slave, back to his master, Philemon; however, Paul also pleads with Philemon to consider Onesimus as a beloved brother in Christ, rather than a slave. In several Pauline letters and in the first correspondence of Peter, a slave was cautioned to obey their master as unto the Lord and not unto man. However, masters were also told to treat their slaves in the same manner and even better, by seeing them as brothers in Christ and not threatening them for God is the Master of all mankind. Paul in his doctrine to the Ephesians teaches about the slave and his master to live in obedience, to do what you do as unto the Lord and not as unto man, not to be man pleasers or with eye service (Ephesians 6:5–9; Colossians 3:26). The emphasis is on Christ Jesus and how we serve Him; we do it as unto the Lord! As Christians and more yet becoming disciples, we must demonstrate the life-changing power of the gospel of Jesus Christ. By the washing of the word, we must be able to fulfill the commandment daily to display attention and discipline toward spiritual things and to defend against errors through apologetics. The dispensation throughout the book of Ephesians is God gives Paul great revelations. God wants to get the house in order. God's dispensation, stewardship, and fellowship bring all of the children of God on one accord: same goals and purpose, the same understanding and application of the word of God, one Lord, one faith, and one baptism because we identify with Christ our Lord by His death empowerment for the present by the resurrection of Jesus Christ.

Galatians 3:26–28 states, "For ye are all the children of God by faith in Christ Jesus. For as many of you as have been baptized into Christ have put on Christ. There is neither Jew nor Greek, there is neither bond nor free, there is neither male nor female; for ye are all one in Christ Jesus." We are sons of God through Christ and distinctions of race, rank, and sexual nature will not hinder our fellowship nor grant special privileges. While being the shortest of Paul's epistles, Philemon is a deep revelation of Christ at work in the lives of Paul and those around him. The tone is one of warming personal friendship rather than apostolic authority. It reveals how Paul gently yet firmly addressed a central issue of the Christian life, namely love through forgiveness, in a very sensitive situation. It presents Paul's influence in action by agreement

The believer's ethical duty and diligence in the marketplace is to perform as though serving the Lord Jesus Christ, even when the workers' counterparts—employers or employees—are according to the flesh, that is, even when the other person is not necessarily a good person or a Christian. Remember that the believer draws our strength from the Lord and his power to be obedient, Paul tactfully yet urgently interceded for Onesimus and expressed complete confidence that Philemon's faith and love would result in restoration. Paul's primary goal was to see Philemon freely embrace the fugitive, Onesimus, as a brother in Christ. He also expressed joy in Philemon's ministry and encouraged him to continue. Paul makes it clear of his desire for Onesimus to stay with him because he has been a great help, but insists that Onesimus go back to Philemon and be reconciled and to make peace. Paul first sought Philemon to forgive Onesimus with the God kind of unconditional love that pardoned and forgave sins that we received through the grace and love of God through Christ Jesus. Paul, in his plea to Philemon, offers to pay the debt that was not his own on behalf of his slave, the sinner, and runaway, Onesimus. This is clearly the work of Jesus on Calvary's cross. Paul's mediation parallels Jesus Christ's ongoing intercession with the Father on our behalf of all people (i.e., all slaves and all sinners).

Philemon represents God the Father and symbolizes the love of God, for the meaning of his name signifies brotherly love, charity, hospitality, and he is also a master; Philemon has individuals obligated to work for him because of their lack of, failure to make up, or just missing the standard of the master in charge. Then we have Onesimus, with such an optimistic meaning to his name that stands for profitable and beneficial, but at this time, Onesimus is anything but profitable; as a matter of fact, he is very much an unprofitable slave, one that has damaged his master's goods and ran away. However, Paul stands in as his mediator, the go-between God and man, our arbitrator, the Lord Jesus, Yeshua Hamasiah. Onesimus, being a runaway sinner like the most of us are or have been, but by the mercies of God through His love and grace redeemed us. Brotherly love often requires practical grace and mercy, and Paul soon comes to this point. He explains the conversion of Onesimus and the slave's new value in the ministry and in the family of Jesus Christ. This transformation with Paul's deep friendship with both men is the basis for a new beginning. The powerful message of the gospel is how one who is alienated is now a beloved brother in Christ as well. Philemon and Onesimus were challenged to show unconditional love that they received through the grace of Jesus in God. The love of the Holy Spirit was definitely active in Paul's ministry and in the life of the church. It is the Holy Spirit who baptizes all believers, whether slave or free. into the body of Christ. and Paul applies this truth to the lives of Philemon and Onesimus. Brotherly love often requires practical grace, mercy, and love, which is the major fruit of the Spirit and is clearly seen all through this epistle. Love's perfect work presents an incredible power of Christ to bring healing to broken lives all over God's green earth. This book is all about reconciliation by making peace, by forgiving, and by pardoning one another's sins, thereby restoring separated and divided relationships especially among believers, Philemon and Onesimus.

CHAPTER 12

The Greatest Is the Servant
Humility Is Greatness
Matthew 23:8–12

> But you, do not be called Rabbi; for One is your Teacher, the Christ, and you are all brethren. Do not call anyone on earth your father; for One is your Father, He who is in heaven. And do not be called master; for One is your Teacher, the Christ. But he who is greatest among you shall be your servant. And whoever exalts himself will be humbled, and he who humbles himself will be exalted.

Jesus warns His disciples against the religious hypocrisy; folks, like the scribes and the Pharisees, who are full of pride and are constantly seeking public attention and praise parading around their piety in the marketplace to win praises from others by wearing their outfits. A phylactery is small leather case, which contained certain Old Testament scriptures, that they wore around their arms and on their forehead, and the borders of their garments filled with tassels showing grandeur. Jesus continued to Warn, His followers about hypocrisies, the fakes, fraud, and phonies, then Jesus put the scribes and the Pharisees on blast, criticizing them for their hypocrisies and their self-righteous practices, being full of outward forms, customs, and protocols but devoid of any inner spiritual truths. Jesus confronts those points in which their hypocrisy reduces the effect of the soundness of their instruction. Jesus refers to their countless rules and regulations, which reduced religion to a burdensome and confusing system of ritual observance that kept people in perpetual bondage exemplified by the desire for places of prominence and titles that suggest superiority. These titles and terms promote a certain respect and lofty attitude behind seeking such recognition that Jesus himself condemns. Jesus tells his disciples as well as us today not to let anyone or anybody call you exalted and puffed-up names or titles that will only enlarge our egos and give us big heads and have us thinking more of ourselves than we do too. As well, Jesus incensed that we call no man master or teacher, for no mortal man will ever know all there is to know. For we are finite; therefore, we know in part, we see in part, we understand in part, things are shadow, dark, and gloomy— very much limited. We cannot completely understand all there is to know and/or explain God by defining Him wholly, absolutely, because God is infinite limitless.

Through Jesus Christ the righteous, we can only know God as the Father of glory and He will reveal the mystery of the true and living God to us here a little and there a little. For man cannot master anything; no matter what you know, it is not enough for the exception of Jesus the Christ only. For knowledge puffs up and it makes one conceited, self-important, and arrogant, but charity—that great gift called *love*—edifies the possessor and builds up due benevolence and compassion with others. For we are all brothers in Christ Jesus, for the scripture tells us to call no man Father that is upon the earth as being God for God is the only Father known to man and his kind. God is the Father of all spiritual and physical life. Because of this paternity, God the Father has a personal and a spiritual relationship with all the children of the world, especially the ones of the household of faith as their heavenly Father, the Author and Creator.

This is the name we call the God of the New Testament. He is Father or Abba. First, let us look at the concept of *father*. Father is the name that explains God's familial relationship to his people (see Matthew 5:16–28), the progenitor of the people, a nourisher, the protector, and an uplifter. As pastors, preachers, and teachers of the gospel, we stand in the Father's place as stewards Caring for God's spiritual children, but we are not the Father, for there is but one real Father and it is God the Father of heaven, the true and only God Father—Father God! Paul, the apostle of Jesus Christ, in 1 Corinthians 4:15, clears up this truth for us, saying, "For though ye have ten thousand instructors in Christ Jesus, yet have ye not many Fathers; for in Christ Jesus I have begotten you through the gospel." Yes, we have had many instructors throughout our lives; we have had teachers from K to 12 and through college from Sunday school to seminary, as lecturers, tutors, coaches, and those that were trainers and mentors. We must not ever forget the numerous sermons and lessons by the preaching of the Gospel of Jesus Christ. However, we will never have a Father like God, for God has begotten us through His precious Holy Spirit in Jesus Christ our Lord. We may all have fathers of the flesh, but God authored the fatherhood concept. God is our Father, the progenitor, the paternal father. We, as earthly fathers, are just that, but God is our Heavenly Father! We, as earthly fathers, are surrogates and stewards of our God the Father's children's. God prohibited the word *father* to be used as a mere title of honor by which the members of the Sanhedrin were doing as were those who exercised religious authority over others. Where the everlasting power and divine nature of God are made manifest in creation. Another paternal name God has for us is Abba, an Aramaic word corresponding with *father* to our current intimate words, *daddy* or *papa*. God wants His people to know that we are His children in a relationship with Him and not a religion. We have a loving, caring, nurturing parent in God. Just a closer and familiar name in the relationship to our God and Father Jesus, use it in the garden of Gethsemane as He prayed in Mark's gospel. Paul links the Christians' cry in Romans 8:15 to a spiritual adoption. Paul also writes in the book of Galatians 4:6. "And because you are sons, God has sent forth the Spirit of His Son into your hearts, crying out Abba, Father."

The same spirit, power, and humility that Jesus had in the garden of Gethsemane is in us the children of God. We are to always stare at the bottom, the basement of being. God has ordained that we base ourselves in all humility. In 2 Chronicles 7:14, God tells Solomon, "If My people, which are called by My name, shall humble themselves, and pray and seek My face and turn from their wicked ways; then will I hear from heaven, and will forgive their sin, and heal their land." It is imperative before we, as human beings and especially as children of God and His people, can approach the throne of the Almighty God to ask of anything. It is that we must begin in the untimed posture prostrate in humility. We must forever humble ourselves. It is our responsibility to take control of our actions to know that God Almighty requires humility. It is demanded throughout the entire Bible with no exception—absolutely none! God will not make us serve or worship Him. You will have to want and desire to do the will of God; humbleness leads to exaltation. All great men and women of God have to first be abased and then know that we need the God of glory, the Father of heaven, the Lord of Hosts, the Master of the universe, and the Great Shepherd of the sheep is on our side.

Daddy, I know I need thee. O how I need thee! If we would examine closely, you would discover why Jesus warns his disciples and us today against the scribes, Pharisees, and all religious leaders, stewards, and ministers of the law, which also I might add is the word of the Lord's. Jesus was speaking to the crowds and to his disciples, the disciplined one, all who followed him, teaching them that the scribes and the Pharisees are sitting in the place of Moses in his seat, saying that they are authorized to interpret the law God gave Moses, and so they were. Nevertheless, Jesus continues to inform the crowd that the scribes, Pharisees, and the teachers of the law must also follow and obey the word of God as they teach God's will and obey.

I have learned to appreciate the awesomeness of this profound God-ordained word that we call obedience; our duty to hear and to do—yes, even to submit, obey like a servant and even as a slave, a wife, a husband, a child. We must all become obedient to someone, howbeit master, Father God Almighty. We are commanded to obey the word of the Lord God; however, it goes on to say do not imitate them in their actions. Because they do not practice what they preach or teach. They are hypocrites, applying heavy burdens and loads on the backs of the people, but they themselves are not willing to help or move with a finger to carry those loads and burdens. Jesus wants us to be aware of what not to do; unlike the scribes and the Pharisees, for they want everything to be seen so that the people will honor them. They make for themselves phylacteries of small strips of parchment paper broader with portions of the law written on them and fasten them with a leather strap, either to their forehead or to the left arm against the heart, to remind the wearers of the duty of keeping the commandment of God in their heads and their hearts as a sign and token that God brought them out of Egypt (Exodus 13:16). This was supposed to have potency as a charm against evils and demonic spirits, but the Pharisees and scribes broadened their phylacteries to be more conspicuous and to show themselves superior over the people; hence, they enlarged the border of their garments and made longer the tassels just to be seen of men. These types of people love and crave the best room and the best seats at every feast, every festival, every party, and every banquet. These folks even reserved for themselves seats in the synagogues and in the churches; they also love to be greeted with much respect and reverence in the marketplaces and have people call them rabbi, father, teacher, master. And still today, there are those in the marketplace out and about calling themselves Reverend So and So or Reverend This and That; your name is not Reverent Bill Johnson, your name is Bill Johnson. We want so badly to be elevated up into high and lofty positions to be revered as doctors, lawyers, and masters that we forget who and what we are. I am so tired of hearing, "You have been elevated"; elevated to what? Elevated to where? Elevated over whom? This is one of the tricks of the enemy, and this is one of many reasons God has ordained my life to this mission and purpose to continue to spotlight and disclose bad and foolish traditions. For we all need to understand, no matter how important we become or what our title may be and how prominent God allows us to become here on these mundane shores, we must balance all that with humility of heart. Whether a king like Nebuchadnezzar, or Pharaoh, or Caesar, and even Nimrod, the mighty hunter, you or I are and will always be a servant, a minister of the Most High God always! For as much is given, much is required, so stay humble, for humility neutralizes our fleshly pride.

Forget the titles that make men haughty, pompous pigs and let no man—absolutely no one—call you exalted superlatives that weaken our flesh nature even more. This creates in us an arrogant attitude and makes us think that we are all that and more than we really are, so let all their praise of us be referred back to God the Father by saying, "To God be the glory" or "Praise the Lord" for all his goodness and his mercy and love.

Please remember that we are just dust, clay, earth, a container, and a vessel that God has put His Holy Spirit in that He might receive all the glory out of our bodies.

For if we humble ourselves under the mighty hand of God, He would not have to abase us because God will humble us so fast, it would make our heads, bodies, and our worlds spin. Jesus said, "Why call Me good, for there is none good but the Father," yet Jesus was sinless and went about doing good. However, He knows that all good things come from God the Father Himself, so all praises be to God! The Bible notifies and enlightens us how to emulate the Great Master Teacher Jesus the Christ and show how He gave God all the glory, the honor, and the praise. God wants the world to know that the way up is down in the kingdom of God; humility must precede and that we take no thought for ourselves, no credit, no praise, and no accolades for absolutely nothing. For all praise, all honor, all glory, all dominion, and all power is to the only wise, true, and living God and our Savior.

Jesus called the scribes and Pharisees hypocrites about fifteen times in the book of Matthews, eight times alone in Matthew chapter 23. More than half, Jesus wanted us to know the severity of stage actors, the hypocrites, the fakes, the frauds, and the phonies. Jesus wants for us to be real and humble which is the only way to exaltation in God's eyes, and that is being a servant and a slave to God and that is being great! Don't get caught up in the titles of who's the boss or who's the chairman or who's the president but get caught up in who's the minister, who's the servant, who's a steward of the Most High, and who's doing the will and the work of God. That is most important of what we need to know. God's will and only His will for we are all equal; we are all brethren. All come from the same God and Father, made of the same dust, so when we are converted, we must strengthen our brothers because we have been reconciled to God; we have become ambassadors of Christ. We are to be reconciled to one another, for if we can't love and esteem each other who we see every day, how then can we love and praise God our Father whom we have never seen? So no matter the title, it just gives us more responsibility, just more of God's will for your life to help more people, the brethren, so to be a servant to men, we must do it as unto the Lord. Subsequently, desire this to be called a servant and even a slave; there is none greater than a servant of God.

Jesus continues to say in verse 10 of chapter 23 that we should not be called or call no man master which is to be interpreted "leader" for no man is truly a bona fide leader for we are all followers of something, somebody, and someone, for we have always asked the trailblazers the question, "What led you to do that?" We subconsciously know that we were led by a power greater than ourselves so we continue to look at Abraham, Isaac, and Jacob and wonder how they did what they did; don't you know it was God the Father, God the Son, and God the Holy Spirit, the power that led them as well as us. You can be for sure they did not go on there; they were not that wise to see ahead, but their wisdom came when they feared and trusted in the Lord God with their whole hearts and they didn't lean to their own understanding, but in all their ways, realized and recognized the Lord their God and acknowledged God, and He directed their path for we are all followers. The Apostle Paul said, "Follow me as I follow Christ," meaning let us learn together that God has Salavic power in Jesus Christ for our victory. It is either God the Father or Satan the liar and deceiver that is supervising us to do what we do, but Christians are followers of Christ called to do the Master's will, for if God wouldn't have called us, we would have no direction, absolutely no guidance or supervision. We would be likened unto Cain, a fugitive and a vagabond, out of the will and presence of God to dwell in the land of wandering (Nod). We want to go with Jesus to be in the presence of a good God, so we must believe and receive and follow the right-now leader sent by Jesus Himself from the Father, the awesome Holy Ghost, our Comforter. So the only true leader and master is Jesus Christ, the head of the Godhead bodily, our Lord, and He leads by His exemplary lifestyle of humility and in strength, in meekness, submission in obedience.

So why are we trying so hard to make ourselves so great? Why do I ask? Do we want to be so popular and rich when Jesus made such an example of how He needed no reputation and humbled himself? We must resist the same urges for pride, and God will lift us up for pride is the arrogance of self-worth without knowing God; God wants us in humility, the strength to control our flesh. Jesus has illustrated for us that we need power from God, for we cannot make it without His controlling power over our life. We have been ambling around for years in religion and in the secular world, saying that old adage, "Self-preservation is the first law of nature," but that is a bunch of hogwash. It sounds good, but it is as selfish as Satan, its author. We have come to know that the first law of nature is man's way of preserving his sinful self; we are to mortify our flesh according to the scripture. That cannot happen because we can't sustain life. All we can do is live it to the best of our ability and to the glory of God. The first law of our natural life is to love the Lord our God with all our heart, soul, and might and our neighbors as ourself. God preserves. We have allowed Satan and his religious cronies (i.e., Pharisees, Scribes, Sadducees, and the so-called leaders of this dark and dying world) to set the standards for us—even to hoodwink us, to beguile and bewitch our understanding of the word of God.

Did you know that every born-again child of God is to know the word of God for themselves like a lawyer knows the law? We all should be a nation of priests and ministers of the gospel, students as well, studying the gospel. Fasting, praying, and meditating on God's word, for our fight is not carnal, but it's spiritual for the pulling down of strongholds by the word of God. For the scripture says, "The word is nigh thee even in your mouth that the word of faith which we preach and speak for life and death is in the power of the tongue." Focus therefore on following the leader, Jesus Christ. His word did not allow anything done through strife that is hatred, envy, and anger as well as vainglory. His word denotes boastfulness and vaunting, but Jesus operated out of lowliness of mind, plainly humility and humbleness. Jesus loved to esteem and lift others up more than himself; that is the mindset we ought to follow. We are all looking for a "Well done" from God the Father, but Jesus did not say, "Well done," "Thou good," or "Faithful master." Did he say rabbi, leader, or reverend? In that case, he did not even say "Father," but he said, "Well done thou good and faithful servant, you have been faithful over a few things, I will make you a ruler over many things." Glory to God for the servant gets the reward—yes, we are servants. I declare that I am a slave of God: sold out, surrendered, and totally dependent on the Master for the rest of my life by my choosing. Hallelujah!

Everything in life has a position and purpose to serve in the service of the Lord our God. Service is a part of everyday life; service is life. Everything we do is associated with serving one another. We service our cars. I enjoyed the church service. They give good service. The police serve and protect. Firemen serve. Postmen serve. The dinner is served. The military serves the country. Maids serve. Banks serve. Cab drivers serve. Dogs serve. Satan serves. Money serves. How can I serve you? Was the service all right? The president serves. Congress must serve. The senate serves, and governors serve. Mayors are servants. Judges serve. Lawyers serve. Deacons are synonymous to a servant. Pastors serve. We serve God, and God serves us. Faith serves. Love serves. Hope serves. The greatest shall serve. Jesus serves. Then we act as if we do not understand the purpose of slavery, stewardship, and servants for this is what, who, and whom we are. We do service consciously and unconsciously for it is our makeup.

Only Slaves Wash Feet
Jesus Washes His Disciples' Feet
John 13:4–5

In light of Jesus approaching death, Jesus wanted to demonstrate to His disciples the full range of His love, and He did this in the most dramatic way He could while the last supper was being served. Jesus being fully God and fully man and aware of the greatness of

His birth, His destiny, and His power, He humbled himself and took on the role of a slave by washing His disciples' feet. Frequent bathing was necessary in the warm climate of the Middle East. In Egypt, Syria, and in the Roman-occupied Israel, slaves washed the dust from the feet of guests when they entered anyone's home. Jesus then got up from the supper table and took off His outer clothing and His cloak. Through this act, Jesus literally and figuratively shows His humiliation in its fullest expression of laying down His life. What Jesus literally did was remove His outer tunic and strip down to His inner tunic. In Israel, Jewish men usually wore an inner tunic and an outer tunic or robe, which is the outer garment; they normally removed the cloak, robe, tunic, outer garment when indoors but kept the inner tunic on. Jesus removed His outer tunic and then wrapped a towel around His waist in this attire; Jesus looked exactly like a slave, for this was the standard apparel and posture for a slave in that day. Need I remind you that Jesus was born in an ox stall and wrapped in swaddling cloths and laid in a manger. He was born into slavery as a suffering servant!

Jesus then poured water into a basin and began to wash His disciples' feet and dry them with the towel that was wrapped around His waist. Not only was Jesus dressed like a slave, but He was also doing the work of a slave. Washing feet was such a menial and tedious job that no teacher would expect His disciples to do such work. No one except Christ Jesus would bring a new concept and teach such a lesson on greatness through humility that would change the way of worship, Christendom, and His disciples because the greatest in the kingdom shall serve. In this gospel, John focuses on what happened when Jesus came to wash Simon Peter's feet, and Peter said to Jesus, "Will You wash my feet? Lord Jesus, You are our master. I will never allow You to serve me as if You were a slave. You shall never wash my feet."

Peter meant well, but Jesus needed to associate with His disciples and with humanity in every possible way. This was a kingdom lesson of paramount proportion that Jesus had to teach of the fundamental cleansing, which He brings by way of His life and death. Therefore, if the Son of Man can do it, so can you, for the servant is not greater than his Master. After Jesus had finished washing their feet, He put on His clothes and asked His disciples, "Do you understand what I have done for you?" They were right to call Jesus their Lord and Teacher, but as such, He should have received service from them; instead, He had served them, doing the most humble of tasks. Jesus then gave them a command that we all need to pay close attention to and listen to repeatedly. That we should also wash one another's feet. This act involves acknowledging that we are slaves and servants of the one whose feet are being washed. However, no one person is to take the servant's role; we all are to take the servant role and wash one another's feet, indicating that everyone washes everyone else's feet. Jesus stresses that this is our obligation, as His disciples, we owe to each other, and it is an ongoing obligation and a perpetual objective. Jesus lets us know that He has already set an example that we should follow. As servants, we are expected to imitate our master. As disciples of Jesus Christ, we are called to be both master and servant; at the same time, each of us would render service and receive services. The concept of service to all, especially to those who are socially beneath us, is foreign to the world that a king, a chief, a ruler, and an emperor serving their subjects would be unheard of. Yet this is what Jesus is asking of us all, His disciples. The command to serve does not come without rewards; for the Word says (13:17) that you are blessed if you do these things. God is the source of all our blessings, and we are at peace with God and with man through obedience.

Greatness Is Serving
Matthew 20:20–28
Key Verses 26–28 NKJV

Yet it shall not be so among you; but whoever desires to become great among you, let him be your servant. And whoever desires to be first among you; let him be your slave, just as the Son of Man did not come to be served, but to serve, and to give His life a ransom for many.

True greatness is measured in terms of service, and Jesus provided the highest standard of service in His sacrificial death, atoning all of humanity through reconciliation, making peace. Jesus modeled the service that He expects from His disciples.

The scandalous request of James and John was succeeded by the similarly scandalous reaction to it of their fellow apostles. Jesus addressed the twelve, therefore, and explained to them what true greatness really consisted of, for it is spiritual. Jesus shows them as well as us today that the kingdom of this world is based on how many people you can control in your fleshly human society. However, it is quite the opposite in the kingdom of God, and Jesus' greatness is predicated on how many people you can help, serve, and assist as we walk alongside them, enabling them to achieve what they need to overcome this old, weak, worldly system.

These lessons clearly let us know that being first in the kingdom of God was not the result of personal ambitions but of divine appointment. God alone would decide who would receive His left and right positions. This world's system is all about exploiting its power and the exploitation of power has ruined our society with powerful men and women who have had very little regard for the people over whom they rule over with selfish ambitions at the cost of others.

Thank God for Jesus that He is and was not like other men but gave to us a good example of godly leadership as the Son of God and became the ransom for many. He died that we might live and have the right to the tree of life through redemption. The Old Testament scripture of Leviticus gives us a gleam at the ransom, deriving for the provision that the ransom paid to set us as slaves free by the propitiation. Jesus's covering and His substitution of one thing for another is an important part of the profession of the suffering servant of the book of Isaiah 53:12.

CHAPTER 13

Man's Best Friend
John 15:9–15 NKJV

As the Father loved Me, I also have loved you; abide in My love. If you keep My commandments, you will abide in My love, just as I have kept My Father's commandments and abide in His love. These things I have spoken to you, that My joy may remain in you, and that your joy may be full. This is My commandment, that you love one another as I have loved you. Greater love has no one than this, than to lay down one's life for his friends. You are My friends if you do whatever I command you. No longer do I call you servants, for a servant does not know what his master is doing; but I have called you friends, for all things that I heard from My Father I have made known to you.

We must recognize and realize as children of God that if we love God, love obeys Jesus' commands and lays our life down for friends as well.

When we abide in Christ, our prayers are effective. We begin to glorify God in our fruitfulness. We demonstrate our discipleship, and our joy becomes full through experiencing Christ's own joy within us. The master-servant and the father-son describes the believers' relationship to Christ and to the Father quite vividly, but none is quite as profound as when Jesus told his disciples, they were His friends; it speaks of mutuality and love.

There was a story of a God-fearing man that had a young son, and his son had a best friend, and the father took his son and his best friend out fishing. While out on the water, the boat capsized and the two boys started to drown. The father was in a dilemma whether to save his son or his son's best friend. The father chose to save the best friend of his son and his son died. Years later, the story came up in a church meeting, and all, including a little boy, asked the now elderly father, "How could you make such a decision not to save your own son?"

And he said, "My son was saved. He believed in the Lord Jesus Christ, he was born again and sanctified. However, his friend was not, and that friend of my son is now your father's little boy and our pastor."

No greater love—the greatest love you can ever have for a friend is to give your life for them, and Jesus said that we are His friends if we do what He commands us to do. Jesus said, "I will no longer call you a servant anymore because servants do not know what their master is doing." Instead Jesus said, "I will call you friends because I will tell you everything that the Father told me." Jesus here in this text is the true vine, the real root, and we are the limbs, the branches. We are to produce that same kind of unselfish love toward one another. The purpose here is to honor and glorify God our Father, to let our light shine that men may see our good work and glorify God as Father in heaven, and we do that by bearing much fruit, and bearing fruit makes us God's children and Jesus's disciples. By showing love, which is the first fruit of the Spirit, we remain in God's love. By obeying his commandments and there are only two to be concerned with: first is to love the Lord thy God with all thy heart, and with all thy soul, and with all thy mind. I like to say with all thy personality. This is the first and greatest commandment, and the second is like unto it: thou shalt love thy neighbor as thyself. Neither narcissism nor egoism, egocentrism, lovers of one's own body, desire, sex from one's self. That's Satan's trick and a lie from the pit of hell. Just as Jesus did; Jesus told us that his joy, which is the second fruit of the Spirit, would be in us; and our joy may be made completely full. This, however, is all done through the love of God, for love is not love until it is given away.

Jesus continues to say, "My commandment is this: that you love one another just as I have loved you, for there is no greater love." You have heard of the Greek word *philos*. It is the root of *Philadelphia* and *Philemon*; all are equivalent to brotherly love, comrade, clansmen, fond friend, dear friend, and/or best friend. When I think of a best friend, I think of David and Jonathan; they had a soulmate friendship, rare and precious. First Samuel 20:17 shows us how Jonathan caused David to vow a vow, because he loved him, for he loved David as he loved his own soul. Who do you know that has a friend like that? Glory to God! David came back in 2 Samuel 1:26 with a song about Jonathan after the death of King Saul and his son Jonathan in war. David said, "I am distressed for you, my brother Jonathan. You have been very pleasant to me. Your love to me was wonderful, surpassing the love of a woman." David and Jonathan were soulmates, friends, best friends. This loving friendship was not eros, nor was it cupid love, but it was by all means philos, transitioning into agape love—the total God kind of love: compassionate, benevolent, charitable, the committed and responsible love of God. This is the love David and Jonathan had; they were willing to die for one another.

In this verse as well as the lead verse, you will discover that there are five stages in the best friend relationship; however, we are going to combine four into two and make three steps, and these are the steps: (1) love and sacrifice, (2) condition, and (3) communication and understanding. These steps are a must in every relationship. Keep these steps on your mind for a moment, for we need to cut to the chase; for some believe the myth that dog is man's best friend because the dog is one of, if not the most popular pet in the history of man and his animals as pets.

The dog ordinarily remains loyal to a considerate master, and because of this, the dog has been called man's best friend. My god, how did that happen? Although dogs can be a good and faithful companion to their owners and masters as well, there are wonderful stories that tell us about dogs' heroic and animal bravery that served in the armed forces and even in wartime, WWI and WWII. Dogs that went into space, risked their lives, and saved people in danger. However, to call a dog man's best friend is stretching it a bit too far. Come on now, that is foolishness. A K9, an animal, your best friend, closer than a brother? Absurd! Ridiculous! A dog cannot really, truly love you nor can a dog really, truly understand the condition; neither can a dog really, truly communicate to you with a literal understanding. A dog is a lower being made to do what you the master tells them to do. Dogs are unintelligent to the human's level, for we have dominion and control over all species and animals, including the dog. The problem is that some dog-loving human beings would wish that some humans would act and obey like dogs, just to be subservient like a dog or a slave to your owner or master. "Come," "go," "sit," "stay," and "fetch" as they shout out commands.

Now we see how some human beings lack in their human relationship with one another and with the Vine; if you cannot love me or your fellow man, you cannot even attempt to love God whom you have never seen, for the relationship with God started horizontally and then vertically. The great command is to love the Lord thy God with thy whole heart and love thy neighbor as thyself; this command was not directed to love dogs! Truly, some have man's best friend spelled backward, it is G-O-D, not d-o-g. Nevertheless, this phenomenon contributed to the insurgency of television and the extended viewing of dog shows like *Rin Tin Tin* in the forties and fifties, *Old Yeller* of the fifties and sixties, *Lassie* of the sixties and seventies, *Huckleberry Hound* and *Snoopy* of the seventies, *Beethoven* in the eighties and nineties, the *One Hundred and One Dalmatians* in the nineties and two thousands. We even believe that all dogs go to heaven, but we will put and send one another, a human being, to hell. Dogs are nice and they are good pets that can fit easily into family life and are sources of genuine delight, but to be man's best friend, they are not!

They cannot be because God is. Our Lord Jesus Christ is reconciling us and making peace, uniting an internal friendship with God the Father again. Glory! Here are the three major steps we need to know to develop and become a friend of God. First, a best friend will demonstrate love/devotion and sacrifice/commitment; if we were to examine the book of John chapter 3, verse 16, it will reveal to you that "God so loved the world"—the human race—"that he gave His only begotten son." In essence, that is love, devotion, sacrifice, and commitment! However, there is another scripture that sustains this theory, and it is found in the book of John 15:13 when Jesus said, "No greater love that a man would lay down his life for his friend." This is the heart and soul of love's devotion and sacrifice, laying down one's life for a friend, the ultimate expression of love and sacrifice. As Christians, moreover, children of God, it is our duty to offer our very own bodies as a life responsible, committed, sanctified, and suitable to God, which is our logical worship and service. Furthermore, in the first book of Samuel chapter 20 verses 16–42, David and Jonathan both sacrifice their own lives to be friends in spite of Saul's jealousy; that's love and sacrifice, devotion and commitment, for love gives and love surrenders and love forgoes for the sake of others.

The second awesome stage to true friendship is its condition: John 3:16 states, "That whosoever believe." That is a prerequisite based on the individual's belief, faith, and trust in Jesus as the Christ, the Son of the living God that He loved us, the world, and sacrificed His life in our stead and also rose from the dead by the power of God. The condition is a part we all must display as believers for it becomes a two-way obligation. Jesus said, "I die, you believe, that's our contract." Since Jonathan made a covenant with the house of David (verse 16). This too is a condition. Looking at John 15:13, Jesus mentions, "My friend, if you do what I command you." That is a condition.

Communication and understanding is the third stage. Jesus said in John 3:16, "We should not perish; but have everlasting life." That is communication and understanding. Jesus, in John 15:13, said, "I have told you everything I heard from My Father."

Augustus Caesar's World /author Genevieve Foster, No Longer Slaves/ author Brad R. Braxton, Slavery in Early Christianity author Jennifer A. Glancy, dFree - Breaking free from financial slavery author DeForest B. Soaries Jr. Surveying Christianity African Roots / author Jimmie D. Compton Jr. , Africa Bible Commentary / author Tokundoh Adeyemo & 70 African Scholars. Compton's Encyclopedia 1985 edition .

Minister Vanzell Howard is the husband of one wife, his high school sweetheart. To God be the glory of thirty-eight years. He's the father of five grown, saved, mature children and five grandchildren. A former Marine, a retired after 30 years from the postal service, Vanzell now enjoys his leisure time and holds the position of associate minister at New Rising Star MBC, where Pastor Christopher D. Holly is his pastor. Vanzell grew up in Detroit, Michigan, where he was influenced by his devoted grandfather, Deacon King Edward Williams (1896), his former pastor, Dr. William Holly (1918). His mentor minister, Ronald Horton (1950). Vanzell also was given street knowledge by his friend and philosopher, Jimmy Ford AKA Mr. Blood (1946)! This book is a twenty-plus years' journey. This book is God given. You're invited to come and share a perspective that you may have never considered.

www.ingramcontent.com/pod-product-compliance
Lightning Source LLC
Chambersburg PA
CBHW020541160726

47991CB00002B/531